PRACTICAL
FLUENCY

CLASSROOM PERSPECTIVES, GRADES K-6

Max Brand & Gayle Brand

Stenhouse Publishers
Portland, Maine

Stenhouse Publishers
www.stenhouse.com

Library of Congress Cataloging-in-Publication Data

Brand, Max, 1958–
    Practical fluency : classroom perspectives, grades K-6 / Max & Gayle Brand.
        p. cm.
    Includes bibliographical references.
    ISBN 1-57110-410-0 (acid-free paper)
    1. Reading (Elementary) 2. Reading comprehension. 3. English language—Composition and exercises—Study and teaching (Elementary) I. Brand, Gayle, 1965– II. Title.

LB1573.7.B72 2006
372.4—dc22   2005057496

Cover and interior design by Sean McGee
Typeset by Sean McGee
Manufactured in the United States of America on acid-free paper
11 10 09 08 07 06 9 8 7 6 5 4 3 2 1

ii

For our patriarchs extraordinaire,
William Brand and James Kerber

CONTENTS

ACKNOWLEDGMENTS

Coauthoring a book and caring for the needs of three restless sons was a task that we could never have pulled off without the cooperation of Jon, Joel, and Max. We are thankful that Max is a patient older brother who took the time to entertain his younger siblings. He always seemed to know when his parents needed a few extra minutes of writing time. We both want to thank our supportive fathers and family. Their encouragement helped us finish this book.

We would like to thank Brenda Power for her magical editing touches that helped us nurture a seed of thought into this book. Her classroom visits and discussions helped us envision this project. Her guiding questions and insights enabled us to reflect on our own teaching, thinking about how we prompt, coach, guide, and scaffold our learners. Because of this, our book captures our teaching and thinking. Brenda, you are a mentor and friend. We feel privileged to have you as an editor.

We want to thank the teaching staffs at Scottish Corners Elementary and Eli Pinney Elementary for thoughtful conversations. We want to thank our principals, Ron Widman and Tom Bates, for their support and trust. Others who deserve our thanks include all the teachers from our past in Columbus Public Schools and Hilliard City Schools—who would have ever thought we would have done this—and the wonderful and creative staff at Stenhouse including Tom and Phillipa, Jay Kilburn, and Doug Kolmar; your behind-the-scenes work ensures that each book represents the author.

Note to Readers

We wrote this book collaboratively to give readers a full range of elementary fluency instruction from Max's intermediate (grade 5) and Gayle's primary (grades 1–2) classrooms. To avoid confusion, the first-person text refers to Max's classroom.

INTRODUCTION

"Those who would look for simple answers to big questions should go for a country walk on a November afternoon, out where the leaves scuffle, squirrels scurry, jays cry havoc, and the fundamental shape of the hills is now revealed."

Hal Borland, *Hal Borland's Twelve Moons of the Year,* 1985

It was the first day of school, a bit past 2:00 P.M., and we were in reading workshop. My fifth-grade students were carefully examining book covers and book jackets and investigating the contents of their new classroom library, searching for a book to read. Tom, my principal, slid into the classroom, whispered that he would like to see me after school, and left as quickly as he arrived. Alarms went off in my head. What trouble could I have possibly caused this early in the school year? Not even a full day had gone by.

Backpacks packed, learning the dismissal ritual, my students were still chatting, observing and inquiring about what to do with the turtle habitat as we lined up. We walked downstairs and entered the commons, students dispersing to buses, parents and younger siblings, finding their way home. My mind wandered from the spirited first day to the imminent chat with Tom.

Tom entered my room, inquired about the first day, and then quickly stated his dilemma. "We have a student who has not been in school since he was four years old. His dad had pulled him out of school because he pushed a chair towards his teacher. Since the father had not had a good school experience, he did not want the same for his only son. Now his son, Aaron, is twelve and will attend school here."

I asked about home-schooling and this halted our talk. Aaron had been with preschool-age children during the school day, and in the evening he had not been receptive to his father's attempts at teaching him how to read, write, or calculate. He had not had anything resembling a home-school education.

I realized that day that Aaron would be the "big question" for me throughout the year. How could I help someone become a fluent reader and writer when fifth grade would be his first experience in school, as well as his first extended experience with reading and writing? How would Aaron converse with his peers about literacy? Those who have simple answers for how to help students become more fluent readers and writers need to face a teaching challenge like Aaron.

What Is Fluency?

What does it mean to be fluent? Fluency to us is accomplishing a task effortlessly. Students are fluent when they complete tasks automatically, fluidly, rapidly, quickly, and accurately. Students learn how to read chunks of meaning—phrases, sentences, paragraphs—as they summarize ideas and anticipate the next thought while their eyes flow across a sea of print. Regie Routman (2003, p. 128) reminds us, ". . . fluency without comprehension is not reading, it is calling words."

We believe fluent reading begins with emergent readers "reading" familiar stories, guided by pictures, and replicating the rhythm, flow, and intonation patterns of the reader they know best (a parent, sibling, teacher, or friend).

Do our students . . .

- Read in meaningful, phrased units?
- Use punctuation to guide their voices and understanding of text?
- Read fluidly from one idea to the next?
- Read using expression, intonation, and emphasis on important word(s)?
- Adjust their reading rate?
- Anticipate what word or idea will come next?
- Reread phrases, clauses, and sentences when self-correcting miscues?
- Reread texts when they tangle their tongues or do not understand what they are reading?

Figure 1.1 Questions for Assessing Reading Fluency

In the primary grades emergent readers learn decoding strategies, but more importantly they learn that reading is about making sense as they make the words on the page sound like they are telling a story or recounting information from a nonfiction text. Students move from oral reading to whisper reading and then on to lip reading as they move towards fluent, silent reading. Finally, students find themselves reading mainly "in their head," as they become confident and competent silent readers.

Intermediate grade students are learning how to read more complex ideas, developing vocabulary skills, and using their background knowledge to connect what they are reading/learning to new ideas. It takes time and practice to become a fluent reader at school and home and to use fluency skills while reading textbooks.

We work from the same principles in building fluency skills in our classrooms—Gayle teaches a multi-age class including grades 1 and 2; I am a fifth-grade teacher. We allow large blocks of time for students to read. While guiding and coaching our students toward fluency, we want them to ask themselves the self-monitoring question, "Does this make sense?" while reading. Allington (2001, p. 79) refers to this thinking as having "a good story line," an important quality of a fluent reader.

Teaching kids to be fluent readers is challenging. When we think of fluency instruction, our definition now includes writing. Experience and research have taught us that reading and writing instruction are intertwined. We teach under the influence of Frank Smith's (1988, p. 23) words, "They must read like a writer in order to write like a writer." We believe that while we are teaching kids to read, we are also teaching them to write, and while writing, our students are learning about reading. This reciprocal relationship is an important idea that underlies our beliefs as we have developed a systematic approach for literacy instruction, including fluency.

Writing Fluency

What is writing fluency? Fluent writing occurs when the writer effortlessly writes words on the page, concentrating on communicating thoughts and ideas. Fluent writers have control of sight words; understand how spelling patterns (onset and rimes), base words, and affixes work as they grapple with their thinking; and occasionally pause to consider word features as they spell a challenging word. Students also have grammar and sequencing skills as they write to communicate, question, recount, report, or persuade. Fluent writing is a challenge for primary-age students and older students that are at risk. They rely on saying words slowly to record sounds, and are still developing a sight vocabulary of written words.

Fluent writing begins with the emergent writer bantering on as they move marker, crayon, pen, or pencil across a blank page, constructing pictures, squiggles, letters, numbers, and, most importantly, a story world. Students learn about how print works as they label pictures and ideas with captions, using temporary spelling. Through the primary grades, children learn high-frequency words, spelling patterns, and the generative nature of spelling as they learn how to write their thinking. Students study the writing craft and learn about a variety of writing genres. They learn by taking notes, crafting drafts, going back and revising, rereading and editing their writing to become fluent writers. "Rereading is the glue that connects the stages of writing" (Fletcher & Portalupi 2001, p. 69). Rereading, thinking about the message being conveyed, considering the audience and the effects of punctuation, spelling, and grammar help our students develop fluent writing skills and strategies.

Do our students . . .

- Write in meaningful, phrased units?
- Use punctuation in their writing as a tool to effectively communicate their ideas?
- Write fluidly from one idea to the next?
- Have a plan for their writing and think ahead to what word or idea will come next?
- Reread their writing orally? Silently?
- Reread their writing to monitor if it makes sense and flows?
- Review punctuation and grammar to see if it helps them communicate their ideas?
- Reread their writing to revise and edit?

Figure 1.2 Questions for Assessing Writing Fluency

Fluent readers have learned how to sample word parts so that they can automatically breeze across lines of print with divided attention, concentrating on the author's message while noticing print when they encounter new or unusual words. Fluent writers craft their ideas and thoughts on paper with only limited thinking about how to spell words.

Teaching Aaron: Discovering the Roots of Reading and Writing Fluency

I knew Aaron would test everything I knew about literacy and teaching as I found ways to help him become a fluent reader and writer. The second day of school Aaron joined our class. I gave him the quick classroom tour and helped him with his personal belongings. We walked to a cluster of desks, and I showed him to his seat, introduced him to Tim, Robbie, and Alex, his cluster

ｊeN B urhs

I ReD ꝊNARTAⱯ⊃L. about KeN ROhs

TFK - I read an article about Ken Burns

Copying

Caps

Space

letter formation - stop/start

Figure 1.3 Writing from Aaron on Ken Burns

mates, and then explained our activities to start the school day. Students had been instructed on the morning message board to read a *Time For Kids* article about Ken Burns, learning about Burns' passion for making documentaries.

Aaron stared at the article, unable to decipher any of the print. I slid a chair next to him, reading the short text to him. Once I had finished reading, I asked Aaron what the article was about. He was dumbfounded by this question, so I turned to his cluster mates and asked the question again. We chatted while Aaron swiveled his head, looking at the other students. Again I prompted Aaron to think about responding to the text by inquiring, "What was this article about?"

This time Aaron responded with, "It was about Ken Burns." "Okay," I thought to myself, "something to work with." I showed Aaron how to put a heading on a paper, noting that he wrote his name in all capital letters, pausing after he formed each one. He copied the date from the board, using many strokes to form each number, reversing the 8 and 2 for the 28th. I used a large sticky note to write his response, "It was about Ken Burns," for him to then copy in his notebook.

I left Aaron and his group so I could circulate around the class and monitor how other students marked and responded to this text, but I noticed how he labored over the task of copying. I made my way back to Aaron's desk to peek at his paper, prior to discussing the article and thinking with the class. I noted that Aaron's writing was shaky. He had trouble forming letters, did not have space between words, and had a reversal in the date. I reflected about ways to include Aaron with his classmates without drawing attention to his limited literacy knowledge. I walked on eggshells as I moved on with the day.

The Basics of Fluency

The starting points for building fluency for Aaron that first day are based on the principles we use for all our students, regardless of age and literacy ability:

- **Fluency instruction needs to be integrated into reading and writing workshops.**
  Aaron was expected to participate in the reading and writing workshops, since he was not pulled out during these instructional times. The challenge was finding appropriate texts for Aaron to read and supporting him as he learned about how words work.

- **Set daily and weekly routines that lead to fluency growth.**
  Students on the second day of school begin to anticipate daily routines

and rituals (read the board for an initial assignment, such as signaling to a *Time For Kids* article or other text) so they can dive into the task. Aaron learned to read the board, encountering repetitive phrases and words each morning. These meaningful phrases guided his actions and helped him to read fluently and make sense of his new classroom world.

- **Use engaging short texts.**
  Brief illustrated texts like those in *Time For Kids* or other newsmagazines for children and poetry or novel excerpts lead to thoughtful conversations and rereading.

- **Establish expectations that the classroom pace will shift throughout the day, with quick bursts of reading and writing to build stamina.**
  The pace of the classroom has to keep moving. When Aaron encountered a challenge, I redirected the question to classmates and expected them to model possible responses.

- **Provide fluency instruction on demand, as needs arise.**
  When Aaron could not read the text I read it for him, knowing that he could understand the content. This allowed him to join in the task at his ability level.

- **Do not always equate fluency with expression or speed.**
  The starting point for building fluency for Aaron was listening to the flow of ideas, understanding the content of the text, and building his language background as he summarized and anticipated ideas.

- **Oral language is the foundation of all literacy learning—opportunities for talk are essential for developing reading and writing fluency.**
  Aaron, his classmates, and I took time to stop and discuss the ideas in texts as well as the author's craft as we continuously built an understanding of how the world works, and how to use both oral and written language as tools for thought.

Aaron loved to tell a good story, and was captivated by all the reading aloud I did each day. Aaron was the student that always asked me to read just one more chapter or had some insight to the plot that the rest of the class had not considered during read-aloud. This was Aaron's entrée into the "Literacy Club." I should not have been surprised when Aaron wrote a poem about his kitty to give to his father for Christmas or when Aaron used his writing workshop time at the beginning of April to complete a piece of nonfiction writing that summarized his learning during a class study about the Iditarod.

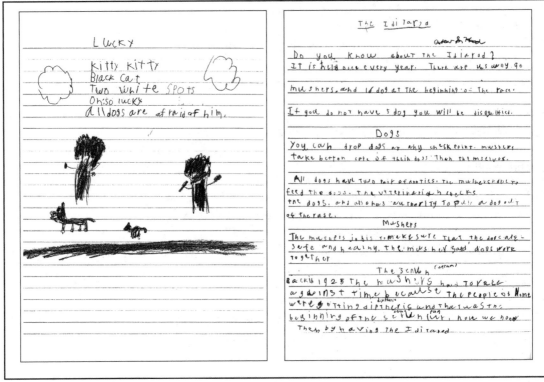

Figure 1.4a and b Aaron's Kitty Poem and Iditarod Writing

Aaron learned the power of language, the use of background knowledge, and a growing awareness of the printer's code to read, write, and think. Aaron began the year able to read his name and the word *the*. Over the course of the year, he read a variety of patterned texts. Aaron developed a reading sight vocabulary, decoding skills, and learned to read for understanding. By the end of the year, Aaron had read from Cynthia Rylant's "Henry and Mudge" series and Arnold Lobel's "Frog and Toad" series. He was able to use his developing sight vocabulary and decoding skills to read sentences, phrases, and paragraphs from grade-level materials with my support.

Aaron was more fluent as a writer than as a reader. He increased his knowledge of frequency words and phonemic awareness. He was able to encode his thoughts and stories on a page. Aaron summarized what he had learned or recounted important information from classroom discussions or reading. Aaron's fluency in writing was ahead of his reading. Even though his skills and strategies were similar to a second-grade student, Aaron could and would participate in grade-level instruction. Aaron's journey into literacy opened our eyes to the importance of fluency instruction and why we teach fluency.

Fluency Instruction

Fluency instruction has been incorporated into our classrooms for as long as we can remember. We know that fluent readers not only sound good, but understand what they are reading. Gayle and I have blocks of time for students to read each day. To develop fluent reading, students need time set aside in each day to read for a variety of purposes. Reading independently without instruction will not ensure fluent reading, writing, or thinking. Questions we have wrestled with for the past twenty years are: *"Who needs fluency instruction?" "Why do they need fluency instruction?" "Why is fluency instruction important?" "What type of instruction do they need?"* Aaron and many students like him have taught us the importance of maintaining our curriculum, yet finding opportunities to guide students implicitly toward greater fluency.

When we plan for instruction, we think about fluency by dividing it into two categories: automaticity with print and phrased reading. According to Pinnell and Fountas (1998), "Flexible, efficient word solving is an essential aspect of both reading and writing processes." Rasinski (1990) reminds us of the importance of phrased reading related to fluency: "Besides being able to decode automatically, fluent readers chunk or parse text into syntactically appropriate units—mainly phrases." We try to balance word-solving strategies with reading meaningful, connected texts. The following are characteristics of automaticity with print and phrased reading we use to monitor students' reading and writing processing as we plan for instruction.

Fostering fluency is a literacy learning goal that we work toward as elementary teachers. We realize that we are not always fluent readers and writers even as literate adults. We read a myriad of texts for a variety of purposes, at times stumbling across the words and ideas, adjusting our reading rate, rereading to understand the author's words. We also stare at a blank page, working to craft personal ideas and thoughts into written words. Students will have these same feelings, tripping over words while reading and having writer's block. Demonstration, thoughtful conversation, and explicit strategy instruction will guide students toward fluent reading and writing. Our goal is to help students understand how to read fluently so they understand what they have read and craft their ideas into written words.

Automaticity with Print

- Knows and uses high frequency words
- Uses beginning letter or cluster to predict an unfamiliar word or write unfamiliar words
- Uses known letter patterns in word to decode an unfamiliar word
- Uses word families to write or decode an unfamiliar word
- Uses syllables to decode unfamiliar words or write unfamiliar words

Figure 1.5 Automaticity with Print

Phrased Reading and Writing

- Students read phrases, using punctuation to guide their reading.
- Students write down thoughts, pausing at the end of sentences or paragraphs.
- Students adjust their reading rate and monitor their understanding.
- Students reread phrases and sentences to decode an unknown word or one supplied by the teacher.
- Students read repeated phrases as meaningful units.
- Students borrow phrases, sentences, and written language patterns from mentor texts.

Figure 1.6 Phrased Reading and Writing

Integrating Fluency in the Midst of Literacy Workshops

From the moment our students arrive at school, there are multiple opportunities to develop new fluency skills. Our daily schedules both begin with an independent reading time. Gayle's first- and second-grade students buddy read, and mine on demand. Students in both our classes read with a friend or in small groups. Gayle's primary-age students often play school by rereading big books or familiar books in baskets. A student often acts as teacher, adopting Gayle's teaching prompts and borrowing her phrases and intonation. Buddy reading and reading on demand accommodates our students' arrival patterns, since they filter into the class over a ten-minute window.

Gayle has an opportunity to greet students, work with small groups of students, have one-on-one conferences, or observe and note student behaviors, depending on the needs of the class. I also greet my students, often listening to snippets of their writing from their writing notebooks that they did for homework. My students read the chalkboard: a greeting followed by directions for their reading. We both gather our students to debrief their first reading of the day, listen to students' news, and outline our plans for the day. Debbie Miller (2002, p. 17) reminds us that teaching "is all about building relationships, establishing

Grades 1–2 Multi-Age	
8:55–9:15	**Buddy Reading**
9:15–9:30	**Gathering Time**
9:30–9:50	**Read-Aloud**
9:50–10:30	**Independent Reading**
10:30–10:45	**Word Study**
10:45–10:55	**Writing Focus Lesson**
10:55–11:30	**Writing Workshop**
11:30–12:15	Lunch and Recess
12:15–12:30	**Read-Aloud**
12:30–1:30	Content Studies
1:30–2:30	Math
2:30–2:40	**Read-Aloud**
2:40–3:15	Related Arts
3:15–3:25	Daily Reflection/Dismissal

Figure 1.7 Gayle's Daily Schedule

trust, creating working literate environments, and getting to know children as readers and learners—and remembering that our classrooms still need to be a joyful place."

A rhythmic clap followed by a greeting is a signal to Gayle's children to put their books away. During this transition, Gayle begins to reread *Mortimer* by Robert Munsch, inviting the group to reading workshop. While students move to the meeting area, they joyfully read the refrain to this well-loved and often-read book. The refrain has been copied onto a piece of chart paper that hangs from the easel next to Gayle. By the time Gayle has finished reading the story, all the children have congregated in the meeting area. Sam, a second-grader, shares that he was like Mortimer last night because he did not want to fall asleep. "I drove my parents craaazy!" Other students begin to share episodes of avoiding bed or going to sleep. Kara, a first-grader, interrupts the conversation to announce, "Robert Munsch got us talking about bedtime again. He does it every time." "That's what good authors do," Gayle affirms and adds, "We talked and thought about some new ways you guys are pestering your parents."

Gayle has adopted the ritual of rereading rhythmic class favorites or singing songs as a transitional tool, motivating her students to join her quickly for read-aloud time. But this is not her only objective. This text, for example, allows her to help children learn about how print works in many ways, as well as digging deeper into its personal meaning.

Gayle's Rereading Fluency Goals

- Enjoy reading
- Demonstrate how to use your voice to show meaning
- Read in meaningful phrases and chunks
- Reread to connect with a text

Figure 1.8 Gayle's Rereading Fluency Goals

Fifth Grade

8:55–9:10	**Reading on Demand**
9:10–9:20	**Debrief/Discuss Reading**
9:20–9:30	**Writing on Demand**
	Students read, reread, reflect, and write about content material. The reading material can be used as a springboard into content inquiries, as well as to build background knowledge for future reading.
9:30–9:45	**First Circle—Plan Day**
	Content Read-Aloud
	Short texts are read aloud to develop background knowledge, trigger questions, and answer questions or as a model to content writing.
9:45–10:30	Content Study/ Inquiry
10:30–11:30	Math
11:30–12:15	Special Areas
12:15–12:30	**Poetry 180**
12:30–1:15	Lunch/Recess
1:15–2:00	**Read-Aloud**
2:00–2:40	**Independent Reading**
2:40–2:50	**Word Study**
2:50–3:30	**Writing Workshop**
3:35	Dismissal

Figure 1.9 Max's Daily Schedule

In my fifth-grade classroom, students enter the room socializing. Then they hang up their book bags, quickly sharpen pencils, turn in homework, and meander to their desks with notebooks and other learning supplies. On the way to their desks, most students stop in front of the chalkboard to read the morning message. It begins with a greeting designed to make them think, and also includes a short reading assignment. This morning the students discover that their reading will be poetry, "Poetry Alive." Students have learned that this prompt asks them to find a poem and reread it many times as they prepare to orally read, using their voices to bring the poem to life for classmates.

The students pull poetry books from the shelf and examine poetry folders to reread drafts, personal published poems, and mentor poems. While reading through the poetry, the students are paying attention to the flow of language in the poems and examining punctuation, word placement, and stanza breaks. They also note poetic conventions as they try to unearth their understanding and the poet's message. Savannah and Alyssa read poems from their writing notebook. They both change the placement of commas and then ask my permission to share their own poems. The girls feel they want to publish these poems and need class feedback as they work on drafts.

After about twenty minutes of searching, reading, rereading, and gladly talking, I ask the children to restore materials and bring something to share with the group. Without prompting, the students sit in a circle, rereading their discoveries, preparing for Poetry Alive.

Poetry Alive is a novel task for students, so I begin by demonstrating how to bring a poem to life. I read aloud "Deer Mouse" from the poetry collection *Turtle in July* by Marilyn Singer. I specifically choose this poem because I know that I have to adjust the speed of my voice to bring Singer's words to life. My voice speeds up and slows down as the mouse of this poem tries to avoid a nocturnal, hovering prey. I read the poem twice. The students have learned that when my demonstration is finished, I will ask them, "What did you notice?" Joseph states that my voice sounded like the mouse's feet—speeding up and slowing down. Megan wonders, "How did you know when to speed up and slow down your voice?" I show the text to the class and reread a portion, demonstrating the importance of space and punctuation in this poem. Before the class wraps around the circle to share their discoveries, Alex asks, "Can we have one more chance to reread our poems? I want to look at the spacing." Alex has chosen to read an Arnold Adoff poem from *Sports Pages* and needs to think about how to bring his discovery to life. After a brief opportunity for revisiting their poems, the students share their morning discoveries and thinking with oral reading and drama. Students provide each other with feedback, ask questions, and applaud each other's efforts while making the morning an effective fluency learning experience.

Max's Goals for His Rereading Demonstration

- Enjoy reading
- Demonstrate how to use voice as a way of demonstrating understanding
- Students practice reading using expressive voices
- Students read in meaningful phrases and chunks
- Students reread to interpret text
- Students assess others' fluency using vocabulary that helps them internalize what it looks like and sounds like to be fluent

---

Figure 1.10 Max's Goals for His Rereading Demonstration

Repeated reading and demonstration are the cornerstones of our fluency instruction. We will continue to demonstrate fluency and the ways it helps readers understand the text they are reading. We will both read aloud every day in our classrooms. Gayle begins reading workshop by reading aloud from the book, *The Other Side* by Jaqueline Woodson. I focus thinking for a science inquiry by reading aloud a short article from a local newspaper, "Plant Powered by Poop." This will provoke questions and provide background knowledge about alternative energy sources and set the tone for their content area reading. Reading aloud will demonstrate the sound of fluent reading. While reading to our students, we will also adjust our reading rate—slowing down to think, examining punctuation, and rereading to make sense of what we are reading. The reading strategies of adjusting our reading rate and rereading are tools fluent readers use to help monitor and uncover new thinking.

Reading and writing workshops are instructional frameworks that enable us to flexibly teach our students to become fluent. We create time each day for multiple read-alouds including fiction, nonfiction, poetry, and student-written texts. We have learned that kid's fluency increases as they engage in more authentic reasons for reading and writing each day and they think more about what they are reading and writing.

How Is This Book Different?

We know there are numerous books published on fluency; we consulted many of them in writing ours. The main difference between our book and most others is that we are classroom teachers. During the past twenty years we have read, discussed, synthesized, and incorporated current research and recommendations into our teaching repertoire. This book provides practical applications of fluency instruction based on research. The underlying structure of our literacy workshop approach includes:

- demonstrating how to accomplish an activity
- providing opportunities to engage in the activity
- using real texts for real purposes
- providing explicit feedback, guidance, and coaching
- providing time for reflection and setting goals

As we shifted our teaching towards supporting fluency, we became more explicit in our teaching, especially with the language we used to prompt student actions. We emphasize fluency work within daily reading and writing and across the curriculum.

We do not overburden ourselves with excessive notes that record students' fluent reading. Instead we have trained our ears to listen for fluent reading during reading conferences. We listen for automaticity as students decode print, noting miscues and their self-repairing strategies. We listen to see if students are reading meaningful phrases, noting when students understand what they are reading or are just sounding smooth. We observe students while they are writing and note spelling and composing strategies. Once we collect this information, we give the students feedback, helping them monitor and set goals for their own growth.

Planning for fluency instruction offers particular challenges for classroom teachers. On a day-to-day basis, fluency instruction requires all of us to use a responsive type of teaching. Observations of classroom anecdotes and informal and formal assessments of students' reading and writing guide our planning for fluency instruction. The school day is packed with opportunities that are ripe for fluency instruction, but how do we capitalize on these moments? Gayle and I are guided by a sense of where our fluency instruction is headed as we explicitly demonstrate fluent reading and writing for our students. Short- and long-term fluency goals guide our instructional moves. By remembering that our kids crawled before they walked, our planning and instruction guides students as they learn to orchestrate the complexities of reading and writing fluently.

READ-ALOUD:
Talk and Text Demonstrations

2

"Reading with fluency every day using all types of text is essential. Students need to hear how fluent readers sound; they need examples of expression and intonation. But students need one more thing: the opportunity to discuss how the reader's fluency affects their understanding of what has been read."

Betsey Shanahan, *OHJELA,* 2004

Recently Joel, our seven-year-old, approached me wondering if I would help him learn how to do a backward dive. Backward dives were the new thing at the pool. Joel was able to easily execute a forward dive and flip with limited gymnastic experience. Now, the daredevil within him took over and he wanted to move beyond these simple tricks to join the "in" diving group, but he was searching for guidance. He couldn't figure this stunt out by himself. Watching the other kids, studying their moves, and talking with them in the diving well were not helping him towards his goal, a back dive. So, when he asked me for assistance, my initial response was silence. Once I had a chance to think about what he was asking, my reflective response was, "How can I help you?"

"I want you to show me what a good back dive looks like. The kids at the pool do them, but they're not that good."

Reflecting on Joel's request and reasoning, I think of the importance of demonstration—helping learners have a clear mental image of what the whole activity looks like. This demonstration not only creates a model in the learner's mind, but supports the ability to envision accomplishing this task. The conversation that surrounds the demonstration is critical. It builds a rationale—the how and why of doing the activity. These are "in-the-head" processes that we take for granted, but need to be explained. Our responsibility as teachers, parents, and mentors is to provide examples and discuss the steps and how they affect the entire activity.

Learning to read and write fluently also requires multiple demonstrations. Reading demonstrations build a rationale for reading fluently, demonstrating how it sounds and how it allows the reader to access meaning within the text. Writing fluently requires demonstrations of the process authors use to move from an idea to words (oral), and then to written language. A first step in building fluency is developing language—both written and conversational. Reading aloud to our students allows us to provide a model of written language, support them as they develop knowledge of common phrases (syntax) and vocabulary, as well as discuss the meaning of a text.

Reading aloud has become an integral part of our fluency instruction. While reading aloud to students we are helping them develop what Holdaway termed the "Literacy Set." According to Holdaway, the literacy set has motivational factors, linguistic factors, operational factors, and orthographic factors. Motivational factors include extensive and repetitive experiences with books and the enjoyment of them. Students are curious about print and love to experiment with it. Linguistic factors involve the grammar, vocabulary, intonation, and idioms of written language. The operational factors are strategies that include self-monitoring, predicting, inferring, and understanding plot structures and the ability to create mental images. The orthographic features refer to print conventions, including the notion that the print carries the message, directionality, left-to-right, top-to-bottom, phonemic awareness, word knowledge, and punctuation. "Children who have developed a strong literacy set begin to operate immediately and automatically in appropriate ways whenever they are faced with print." (Holdaway 1979, p. 49)

While we are reading aloud to our students, we are helping them build linguistic characteristics, book language. Ehri (1998) pointed out that "students need to become familiar with the syntax or grammatical function of the words and phrases they are reading and with their meaning." Readers use grammatical structures and the flow of written language as they anticipate the next word while reading. They are building language patterns, internalizing phrases, learning about the probability of the next word in a sequence of written language. Students also develop story structures, plot, cause-and-effect relationships, and other formats of written language. While we are reading aloud, we are also helping our students develop motivational and operational factors and showing them orthographic factors.

We read aloud entire texts, picture books, novels, poetry, passages from nonfiction trade books, and articles as we help our students understand written-language grammar. We want them to understand the relationship of meaning to the structure of written texts. Students build an understanding that syntax is not removed from meaning—as we fluently move through a text, readers predict based on an understanding or need to understand. Most of our students understand this concept as it relates to oral language, but some do not use it while reading. Reading aloud becomes central in demonstrating this fluent reading behavior.

We both challenge ourselves to find time in our busy daily schedules to read aloud in our classrooms, usually three times a day. Reading aloud to our students is a ritual that we include in our daily plans because of our love for literature and poetry and the discovery that happens while exploring the world of nonfiction texts. Those odd few minutes prior to special areas, lunch, and the end of the day are wonderful for rereading snippets of language as we try to keep demonstrating fluent reading behaviors and develop students' language skills.

Our daily plans include a time for reading fiction, nonfiction, and poetry. While demonstrating the sound of fluent reading, we prompt our students: *Listen to how smooth my voice sounds. Notice how I read the punctuation.* Instruction is explicit, calling attention to our fluent reading and the punctuation that is guiding the fluent reading. This explicit instruction helps accelerate our students' fluency understanding. We also think aloud to illustrate how we infer and summarize what we are learning from the text. This thinking allows us to anticipate or predict what ideas may come next and helps us read fluently. The prompts and thinking will be used in other reading and learning contexts.

Reading aloud provides us with opportunities to help students develop language and thinking skills and know what it sounds like to be fluent. These teachable moments help support our students' development of fluency, as well as reading and thinking strategies. But we continue to help students, even intermediate-age learners, develop oral language while helping them develop book language (grammar), common phrases, and sayings.

Reading aloud not only provides a model for the sound of fluent reading such as adjusting reading rates and rereading, but also helps students understand the importance of phrased, fluent reading. When students listen to a story or text read aloud, they begin to fill in gaps. They summarize and synthesize information and begin to predict words, phrases, and ideas, a critical skill for fluent readers. Students who have had many opportunities to hear stories read to them begin to internalize the rhythm and flow of written language. Since the text is being read to them, students' minds are free to focus on the meaning and structure of the story language.

We use the same cueing system to prompt our students in reading independently. So, when we use the prompts *Does that make sense?* or *Reread that sentence and think if it makes sense,* the readers understand that the prompt is asking them to monitor the meaning of the text—a critical understanding we need to constantly reinforce for students struggling to read fluently.

When planning for fluency instruction by using read-aloud, we consider our students' needs. These questions help us focus our read-aloud time to support fluency.

Planning for Read-Aloud

- Do students use the meaning of the story to anticipate the next word or idea?

- Do students use the meaning of the text and punctuation to guide their intonation?

- Do students monitor when they do not understand the text?

- Do students reread to help them infer the meaning of a text or self-correct a miscue?

- Do students adjust the pace of their reading?

Figure 2.1 Planning for Read-Aloud

Read-Aloud

Read-aloud is the glue that binds all of our literacy instruction together, but more importantly to us, it helps build community. During read-aloud time, students interact with us, their classmates, and a variety of texts, becoming members of what Frank Smith (1988, p. 3) called "The Literacy Club." Smith reminds us that an advantage to membership in The Literacy Club is "relevant assistance, and differences in ability and interests are expected." Students like Aaron, Jenna, Sylvia, and Joseph that have come to fifth grade not reading at grade level can still thoughtfully discuss and learn from grade-level materials. By reading aloud to students and demonstrating fluent reading, we are providing a model of a fluent reader and also providing access to the world of these challenging texts. Students enjoy stories, learn about the world, and integrate book language into their thinking as they understand the importance of reading and writing in their lives.

Print features (sentences, phrases, words, and punctuation) are critical to helping our students untangle their confusions while developing automaticity and fluent reading and writing. Examining sentences and phrases that are meaningful is a good starting place. The sentences and phrases that we take a closer look at are the ones students want repeated, the ones that make them stop and think, or ones that we feel will teach our students about an aspect of print that confuses them. We talk about end punctuation of sentences as a chance to think, summarize, question, and think what may come next. We also discuss the importance of internal punctuation (commas, colons, and semi-colons) and how the ideas are connected. In the wonderful book *Eats, Shoots & Leaves,* Lynne Truss (2003, p. 71) makes the point, "On the page, punctuation performs its grammatical function, but in the mind of the reader it does more than that. It tells the reader how to hum the tune." This is the same tune we want our students to notice while reading, becoming fluent. To support this thinking we ask students to "*Listen for the punctuation while I read. Why do you think the author wrote it this way?*"

To enhance this teaching, we copy sections of a read-aloud text and ask students to read along, noting the use of punctuation as it relates to meaning. In Gayle's primary classroom she uses big books and poetry on the overhead to accomplish this objective. Gayle has noticed that her students are reading through end punctuation and not pausing at commas. They are reading quickly not fluently. Her focus lesson for reading workshop will focus on using punctuation to help students read fluently, not quickly.

Gayle places the big book *The Jigaree* (Cowley, 1983) on the easel as her students store the books used during buddy reading. "This morning we are going to reread *The Jigaree.* When listening to many of you read, I have noticed that you're reading fast, not fluently. We are forgetting to use punctuation. Joy Cowley has used commas and periods to help us read fluently. Listen to me read this first page, notice how my voice pauses at commas and stops briefly at periods." She reads the first page, demonstrating fluent reading.

This is a good text to demonstrate fluent reading. The text uses a rhyme pattern so that the last word of each line automatically spills from your mouth. This book is a patterned text that primary-age students will read over and over. The use of periods and commas help the reader and make it easy for children to learn how to read these punctuation marks.

When she finishes reading the first page she asks her class, "What did you notice about my reading?" Bailey comments, "It sounded almost like you were singing a song." "Yeah, you read the first part all together and only took a short breath at the first period," Ellie reflects. Kara adds, "It seems like when you read 'jumping here, jumping there,' you paused at the commas so you could get your breath to say the next line, just like we do in music." "I'm glad you noticed. That is exactly what I tried to do and what I want you to help me do when finishing this book together."

Gayle and her class finish reading together, commenting periodically on how smooth they sound. When the students are sent off to read independently during reading workshop, Gayle reminds them to pay attention to punctuation. "Use it to help you sing the words in your head." This simple metaphor will be a reminder and a prompt Gayle uses with her students in other shared reading experiences such as reading aloud and small-group work, and as part of individual reading conferences.

I may copy a portion of a text or poem on chart paper or use on the overhead to highlight how to read punctuation. For example, prior to reading the poem *The Night Before Fishing Season Opens* by Don Graves, I copy the text on a chart for all my students to view.

> After supper, Dad helps
> George and me check the supplies:
> creel, bait tin, worms, pole,
> rubber boots, not used
> since last summer.
> I see orange-bellied trout
> dancing on the brook bank.
>
> 8:00 P.M.
> Lay out my clothes
> and wait for dawn:
> burrowed into my pillow
> hoping for sleep;
> beneath the waterfall,
> a pool boils
> with hungry trout.
>
> 9:00 P.M.
> Flip my pillow

to the cool side.
Cast my line
under the bridge, feel
the rat-a-tat of trout bites,
a quick jerk to set the hook.
I play the brookie to shore,
catch the speckled flash
of color before I swing
him to the bank.

9:40 P.M.
I imagine Mother's call
and smell the bacon;
bounce to the floor
and one by one I put on the clothes
from the neat pile
on the chair:
trousers, shirt, jacket.
I sit down,
slip on my long socks;
reach for my boots.

After my second reading of the poem, T.J. turns to Ben and asks him so that we all can hear, "Did you get it?" Ben's response is emphatic, "No." Nathan admits that he is a little confused himself. I thank them for their honesty and probe, "What don't you get?" "All the stuff he says about seeing and catching fish. I thought this was about the night before fishing? It seems like Don Graves has some mixed-up thinking in this one," Nathan responds. T.J. answers my monitoring question with, "He lost me in the second sentence." Maggie joins in by stating, "T.J., the first time Mr. Brand read the poem I was confused, but then I noticed that Don Graves is using punctuation to separate ideas."

"I still don't get it," Savannah says to Maggie. She asks me to read the first stanza again. I reread the first stanza, grouping ideas together, stopping for an extra second before reading the last sentence. When I'm finished reading the first stanza, T.J. says, "I get it. Don is using periods and colons to help us understand how hard it is to go to sleep." Ryan looks at Savannah and says, "Listen to the second stanza. I'll read it and make it seem like he is rolling in his sleep." We chorally read the last two stanzas the way Ryan has demonstrated, like we're rolling in bed.

I bring closure to the lesson by asking, "What did you learn today?" Claire states, "I need to reread when poems don't make sense. I don't always look at the punctuation; it seems easier to read line by line." Nathan agrees, adding, "I need to slow my reading down and pay attention to colons and semi-colons." As we prepare for lunch, Jessica whispers to me, "I never knew what those marks were," referring to the colon and semi-colons. Reflecting on the lesson, I realize that it is important to not only name punctuation, but show how it helps the writer talk to the reader. I will plan more lessons where the kids have to use punctuation in both their reading and writing. I will also need to have the students collect examples of commas, colons, and semi-colons so that they understand how to use them in their writing and reading.

While focusing on print features, I am careful to demonstrate how these marks help me understand what I am reading and how to use them while writing. Teaching the purpose of punctuation, and not just the names of the marks, helps students to use punctuation thoughtfully in their own writing. Gayle's students favorite use of punctuation is an ellipse, those three dots that they have noticed in a myriad of texts. It is not the naming that is important for these young learners (although they love to use an adult sounding word), it is using it in their own writing and then celebrating about how wise they are to use this writing tool in their own texts.

Extending our teaching from lines of print to page layout and format, I may choose a book like *Sea Clocks: The Story of Longitude* by Louise Borden (2004) while Gayle may use *Diary of a Worm* by Doreen Cronin (2003). These books are both nonfiction texts. *Sea Clocks* is an informational text that tells the story of how John Harrison used a sea clock to measure longitude. *Diary of a Worm* is an informational book that provides information about a worm from its perspective, using a diary format. These books present interesting concepts and have interesting text formats and page layouts. They open kids' minds to wonder, reread, and discuss the ideas and concepts. Teaching students how to orient themselves to texts builds background knowledge and supports students' fluency. A recent study found that "picture walks were effective in promoting fluency" (Stahl, 2003). Since previewing a text is a habit we want our students to use independently, we demonstrate it explicitly.

Sea Clocks

When reading aloud to our students we both preview books similarly. First, we read aloud the title as we examine the book, noticing the picture, back cover, and inside flap. We may state the title a few times, letting the words sink in.

While thinking out loud, we set a purpose for our reading. The purpose may be stated in question form. I like to write my purpose or questions on a piece of chart paper, demonstrating how students can organize their own notebooks. Our goal for previewing is to show students how activating schema prepares us to think about our reading.

While I am reading aloud, the students are sitting in a circle with their reading notebooks. Students use a reading notebook to set a purpose for my reading. They also use their notebooks to ask questions, predict what they think will happen next, draw sketches that reflect their understanding, and record interesting words and lines of text as we work together to understand the text. Each day we also chart our thinking as we think through picture books or a novel. The chart is a tool for recording important words and lines and our thinking. While writing on the chart, I can demonstrate concepts about fluency that students cannot glean from only listening to the sounds of text. While writing words on the chart, I can also support important word learning concepts such as focusing attention on consonant clusters, how words sound, and what they look like. We can also explore important decoding strategies used by fluent readers and encoding strategies used by fluent writers.

While beginning to read *Sea Clocks,* I wonder how clocks on ships were used to help determine lines of longitude. During the demonstration, Cole inquires, "When were clocks invented?" Brock continues the same thread of thought with a question, "I wonder how hard it is to keep accurate time at sea?" Maureen joins the thinking by stating, "I didn't think they kept time on ships. I thought sailors kept track of days." Typical of most of my read-aloud demonstrations, my students take ownership and think along with me. I continue my demonstration, saying, "These are important things we need to think about while setting a purpose for reading this book. My purpose for reading *Sea Clocks* is to learn how clocks helped sailors determine lines of longitude. I also wonder why there was a need for lines of longitude." On the top of a piece of chart paper I record the purpose for our reading. We reread it; Alex thinks it is important that we are wondering because she has adopted questions for setting her own purposes during independent and content area reading.

I read the entire text out loud to the class. With each turn of the page we examine the layout and pictures, thinking about how this narrative recounting is put together. We look at the text layout, asking, "Why did Louise Borden use this format to tell her story? How do these text pictures support the narrative? How are they helping us read big ideas?" While reading I periodically stop, summarize what I have learned, jot a quick note on the chart, and then predict what idea will be presented next as I anticipate the story line. The movement of time in this text is intriguing as years move ahead without any narration.

We dig deep into the text, trying to understand the challenging concept of longitude. Aaron tries to help by adding his knowledge of Greenwich Mean Time, the prime meridian, and the equator. The author's note and interesting facts about John Harrison's life captivate the class. We revisit this section of the book, thinking about Louise Borden's ability to take a little piece of history and create a wonderful story. Aaron and Tim ask for the book so they can explore it further during independent reading time.

When the read-aloud is finished, I ask the kids to talk about how previewing, setting a purpose, summarizing, predicting, and revising my/our thinking helped them understand the text and how my fluent reading, especially slowing down and speeding up, assisted their comprehension. Ben comments that he noticed I varied my reading pace, sometimes rereading two or three times when the information was not clear. Alyssa remarks, "Sometimes you read fast, making it sound like a story. Sometimes I got bored. It is the same with my social studies text. It can't all sound like a story. I need to pay attention to the information; setting a purpose and summarizing helped you and could help me." Dylan adds to both kids' observations, "You read important parts real slow, maybe too slow for me, but this was important junk." Paxson admits, "I probably need to read at different speeds, I read everything fast, trying to be done first. Sometimes I miss some important information, especially in pictures and captions."

Nonfiction Reading Anchor Chart

- We can preview a text by reading the title, examining the pictures, back cover, and inside flaps.
- We can preview a text by looking at pictures and diagrams by reading captions.
- We can look at text features to develop background knowledge and schema.
- We can set a purpose for our reading.
- We can adjust the speed at which we read. When the text is confusing, slow down.
- We can pay attention to punctuation, reading the text and ideas the way the author wrote them.
- We can reread when we are not sure what something means.

Figure 2.2 **Nonfiction Reading Anchor Chart**

Building fluency and reading pace vocabulary with the group, I summarize their observations, "I adjusted my reading pace because there were times that the text was challenging to understand. This is when I slowed down, summarized, and had to use my schema to think about my background information and use the text layout. Other times I enjoyed the story and read the ideas, using the punctuation to guide my reading." The demonstration ends with discussion about how the students will use what they learned from this lesson, as well as other demonstrations that may help them develop fluent thought.

This lesson and others like it helped the students read more carefully from content reading materials including their textbooks. The students previewed texts carefully, setting purposes for their reading, and then adjusted their pace based on their purpose. Students did not get bogged down while reading and used text features as background knowledge while reading. Paxson, a voracious reader, challenged himself to vary his reading pace and reread information as one of his quarterly reading goals. Alyssa's goals were to read more quickly, not getting caught up in the details that slowed her reading pace down and often confused her. Since my students are aware of each other's goals, Paxson and Alyssa buddy read, supporting each other as they worked towards their reading goals and understanding what they read.

The Diary of a Worm

Gayle previews the book by looking at the front cover, turning the book over and examining the back of the book. She thinks out loud about what she knows about a diary and that it's personal, often written in first person. "This means I may be a word used a lot. Maybe it will have statements that begin with 'I like' or 'I think,'" she tells the group. Surprisingly, these first- and second-graders are quiet, letting her thinking sink in. Gayle sets a purpose by stating, "I'm going to read this book to find out what a worm's life is like." John challenges her by saying, "I disagree, this is going to be a made-up story, look at the picture. That is just a catchy title." Gayle asks her class to turn and talk to each other, "Set a purpose for reading this text." After a few minutes of small-group talk the group decides that, "We are going to read the book to decide how the title goes with the story."

Gayle reads aloud *The Diary of a Worm*, demonstrating how she is using the date of the diary, what she knows about diaries and worms to predict what will come next in the story. She reads the text, noting punctuation and the format of the text. She varies her pace, and calls attention to this strategy. She tells the group that not only did she slow down, but also reread that part, trying to understand the information.

This book is added to a basket of the most recent read-aloud books, and students will have multiple opportunities to revisit this text during independent and buddy reading times. Books placed in this basket are also reread during the few odd minutes in Gayle's day. Tommy and Bailey also studied this book during writing workshop, creating *An Ant's Diary* based on the structure of this text.

She concludes her demonstrations with a reflection time, charting student insights on an anchor chart. The anchor chart is reread by students as they independently read or Gayle reads aloud. This reference chart anchors students thinking as they preview their own reading materials during independent reading, small-group instruction, or shared reading situations.

The sound of a fluent reader is demonstrated during each oral reading experience. We both rely on the prompt, *"Listen to how I sound when I read this."* This prompt asks the students to focus their attention on our voice, noting rhythm, flow, and meter. We follow up the oral reading with the monitoring question, *"What did you notice?"* This asks students to notice how expressive voicing makes the story come alive, similar to oral story telling. Discussions often highlight the importance of reading chunks (sentences, phrases, punctuation) that are connected and point out how groups of related thoughts flow together. This helps the reader understand what they are reading and predict what may come next. We are developing schema for text structures. We also take time to point out print features.

Students are interested in lines of text for a variety of reasons. I often reread these lines and record them on our class chart. While writing them, I can demonstrate fluent reading by writing phrases and then pointing out the punctuation the author has used. Students often copy these phrases and sentences into their own reading notebooks. They reread these wondrous words one more time, copy them as phrased units, learn about how punctuation works, and internalize written language.

These lines are read over and over again by students—on anchor charts, on walls, and in their notebooks, and it becomes shared language in the classroom. Students reread their notebook pages as they set purposes for the day's read-aloud, using lines from their own notebooks, daily anchor charts, or the word wall to shape their thinking. These lines of text become part of the students' language, incorporating the vocabulary as their own, and developing fluency as they reread these lines of text, digging deeper into the author's meaning.

The first lines that find their way to our class word wall come from read-aloud. Lines that the group feels represent interesting ideas are posted on

28

sentence strips, displayed on the word wall under the heading "lines that make you stop and think." They are reread as students notice relationships between ideas across texts. At the end of the year my students identified the lines we reread and referred to most often:

> "If someone looks into your eyes, I read in a book one time, he'll see right into your soul." From *Pictures of Hollis Woods* (*Giff* 2002)
> "Hate just creates more hate." And "I guess you never know about people." From *Belle Teal* (*Martin* 2001)
> "Don't you think it is odd that Mrs. Partridge, who is blind, could see something about me—but I, who could see, was blind about her?" From *Walk Two Moons* (*Creech* 1996)

These are interesting lines of thinking that students may overlook without guidance. We reread these lines to make connections across texts, as mentor lines for writing, or to decide if they were worthy of public display, which led to discussions about punctuation and the importance of fluent reading. My students often reflect that reading aloud and using their notebooks and the word wall are the tools that help them realize the importance of fluent reading in understanding what they read and how they write.

At the beginning of the year I spend time demonstrating how to notice features of texts that enable my reading to be fluent so I can try to understand them. Once students internalize the importance of an activity, they guide my thinking, requesting lines of text to be written on the chart. When I read the class *Saturdays and Teacakes* by Lester Laminack students guide me as to what to record on the chart while they use their notebooks.

"Hey, Mr. Brand you better write 'Every Saturday' on the chart. He repeats that phrase. This story must have happened a lot," Tim informs me and his classmates.

I continue reading when Alex breaks the spell of the story, "Read that line again." I reread the line, "In our little town everyone knew everybody . . . and told everything to anyone who would listen." Alex and Maggie insist that line should go on the chart because that idea is like the thinking from *Belle Teal* and *Hidden Roots* (*Bruchac* 2004). As I write the line on the chart, Alyssa asks, "Why isn't there a comma after the word 'town'? It sounded like there should be one the way you read it." Robbie, thinking out loud, says, "I think there isn't a comma because 'everyone knew everybody' goes along with 'our little town.'" Paxson agrees with Robbie and reads the line without pausing like I did, demonstrating how the ideas flow together.

We finish reading the story, pausing to record interesting words and lines on our class chart. Not all the students' notebooks look the same. The read-aloud, notebooks, and chart are springboards for demonstrations, conversation, and reflection as the students learn to read like writers.

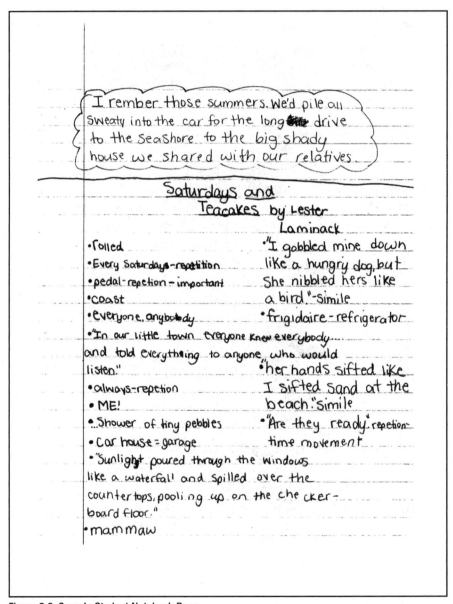

Figure 2.3 Sample Student Notebook Page

Cloze Procedure

While we are reading aloud our students are learning about written language such as common phrases and word possibilities, and they are summarizing ideas and thinking in meaningful units, characteristics of fluent readers. Fluent readers are thinking ahead, anticipating ideas and words they may encounter. Another way we build fluency is to scaffold students' predictions, encouraging them to anticipate while we are reading aloud. Oral cloze procedure (leaving a word out) is how we begin this type of instruction. Reading aloud using an oral cloze procedure is something that I may do with my fifth-graders as a mini-lesson at the beginning of word study block or use a familiar book or excerpt that I read in the few odd minutes that pop up in my day. Gayle is a bit more systematic in her planning, using a short stretch of time at the end of her morning or before her kids go to related arts.

While reading aloud, we leave a word out, asking students to fill in the missing word. This is based on Holdaway's thinking (1979, p. 101), "The easiest way of inducing meaningful language activity is to provide gaps in an otherwise complete flow of language. No one can resist it. In reading, this impulse is almost as strong as it is in listening—and it has obvious implications in talking and writing. Gap-filling requires the responder to be sensitive to all linguistic constraints operating in the context, and it is therefore possible to control very delicately the nature of the induced language activity, or skill, by selecting the nature of the gap and the nature of any cues which may be allowed to stand within it."

Students grow into the habit of calling out a left-out word. We have found that many of our students that struggle with fluency are not using the meaning of what they are reading and the structure of language to help them think ahead. We want to guide and build this thinking, teaching students how to use their language background while reading.

Since filling the linguistic holes is something that the mind does spontaneously, we capitalize on this linguistic strategy. We do not need lengthy demonstrations to introduce this thinking. Instead, we talk with our students about how they are already thinking about the next word we are going to say even before it comes out of our mouths. One example is how much easier it is for them to predict the next word in an activity we do each day, especially if we use the same prompts and questions. Heads nod as they understand.

Since many of our students have played guessing games similar to this at home, and even while being read to, we move on and discuss how to predict. We refer to background information and summary skills. So, when we try this with a predictable picture book or familiar text, children have little difficulty filling in missing words. If they miscue, their approximations make sense, which is exactly the strategy we are trying to induce in our disfluent readers.

Gayle has left five minutes in her morning to reread Don and Audrey Wood's *The Little Mouse, The Red Ripe Strawberry, and THE BIG HUNGRY BEAR*, guiding her students to "fill in the gaps when she leaves out words." This class favorite has a memorable text that students have internalized and is meant to be read aloud with fluency, especially where there is dialogue. (Books written by Robert Munsch also lend themselves to this type of instruction.) There are many places that Gayle could leave gaps in the text, but her goal today is for her students to use the repetitious phrases and flow of the text to maintain fluency. Dropping her voice off at the phrases "red, ripe strawberries & big, hungry bear" help her students read ahead and group ideas as meaningful phrases. During previous readings of this text, she has discussed the comma usage and how it affects her reading. This short, focused instruction is grounded in her assessment of snippets of oral reading during today's reading workshop.

The pacing of this instruction is fast, with short interludes to emphasize the fluent reading strategy. There is little discussion about the story (a familiar one), since our goal is to build an automatic processing system. The flow of the text replicates Gayle's fluency goal and helps her students anticipate and fill in the gaps in the text. Once students have been introduced to this idea during read-aloud, it becomes a teaching strategy we use during small-group fluency instruction and individual reading conferences.

Masking Words

Once students have become comfortable with oral cloze procedures, we extend this instruction by writing portions of familiar texts on a chart or overhead and masking or leaving out a targeted word. Big books are another resource that Gayle uses.

32

Masking Decisions

- Rhyming words
- Show first letter
- Show beginning blend
- Mask vowel
- Show first syllable
- Show first word of a compound word

Figure 2.4 Masking Decisions

Our goal is to train students' eyes to work with their ears by reading ahead, thinking about word possibilities, and developing automaticity. When making masking decisions, we use miscue analysis to decide what portion of a word to mask. We may leave an entire word out, revealing a blank space for students to fill in. Beginning with rhyming words helps the child use the structure of the text to fill in the gap. This is parallel to word-building lessons, which emphasize how to manipulate onsets and rime (word families).

We may reveal word parts, if our miscue analysis reveals that our students are not fluent because they are having difficulty using the beginning of words to decode unknown words. This procedure reinforces reading in phrases and becomes automatic with word-solving strategies. Parts of a word are shown so that students learn how to use specific word features in a text, along with using meanings. Students may also need to reread the text, think about the meaning of the text, and use this information to decode the print. We demonstrate the importance of rereading not only for decoding purposes, but to dig deeper, to try to understand the text.

My fifth-grade students fan out across the classroom, finding a quiet and comfortable spot to read independently. I invite Jessica, Jenna, Joseph, and T.J. over, meeting in front of the easel. I have copied the poem *Rabbit* (Graves 1996) on a piece of chart paper, masking a few words for the students to problem-solve while reading fluently. My goal for this group is to have them use the meaning and structure of their reading to help them predict what word could come next. I will only reveal the first letter to the group because they have a tendency to "sound it out."

"When I read this poem I want you to think what word looks and sounds right where I have left blanks," I coach the group. I read aloud the first stanza, while the students follow along. I change the intonation of my voice to

---

Rabbit

"Hey, Rabbit, come here."
I am the new kid
In the fourth grade.
My ears grow warm and large.

Sometimes I look
at them in the m_ _ _ _ _
but not for long.
My dad says, "Heavens,
He's got ears just like me."

In the spring, Jimmy and me
b_ _ _ _ a hut in the woods
and he says,
"Hey Rabbit, you b_ _ _ _
cool huts; how'd you know
how to do that?"

That night
after I brush my teeth,
I take another look
at my ears and I think
maybe they've shr _ _ _.

Figure 2.5 Masking Decisions

33

read the first line, making it sound like the voice is mocking the character. This brings a chuckle from the group. When I read the second stanza and come to the first masked word, I drop my voice out, letting the group problem-solve. "M,m,m" is Jessica's first attempt. T.J. thinks they should read on. Jenna wants to reread. Joseph whispers, "Mirror, yea, mirror." "What?" T.J. asks. Jenna and Jessica reread the first part of the sentence inserting *mirror,* continue to the end of the sentence and then agree with Joseph. I fill in the missing letters of *mirror* in blank spaces. "It is *mirror* T.J., they are talking about his ears," says Jessica. We reread it one more time with the word filled in.

I continue reading; the group joins me, chorally reading now. Again I drop my voice out at the second masked word. To my surprise T.J. reads *build* and plows ahead of the other three. When the stanza has been reread by the group, Jessica asks T.J. how he knew the word so quickly. He responds by saying, "I cheated, I read ahead and figured it out by looking at *hut.* They were building a hut in the woods." I fill in the blanks while the kids discuss their thinking, and then reread the stanza. The last stanza is read and the students read *shrunk,* understanding that Jimmy thinks he is OK, so his ears must have shrunk to the size of a typical fourth-grader.

We chorally reread the text. Joseph asks if he can have a copy of this poem for his poetry folder, he thinks his dad would enjoy the poem. I finish the lesson by asking the group how this will help them when they read independently. Jenna reflects, "I'm going to read on, think about what the story is about. I sound out too many words." T.J., laughing, agrees with Jenna. The students join their classmates for independent reading. I will pull the group together tomorrow for a similar lesson and then confer with them in a day or two, listening for the effect of my lesson on their reading.

Text Innovations

In 2002 we both heard Shelley Harwayne speak at a Reading Recovery conference about text innovation. Shelley was referring to using text as a model for writing. When students use text innovation as a writing strategy, they often change one word from a sentence, typically either a noun or verb. We are always working to help our students develop written language patterns. Even though we used text innovation successfully as a teaching strategy, we felt that maybe our instruction moved too fast and excluded or confused some children. One teaching method that has helped students understand this strategy is their oral rehearsal or "writing in the air." Shelley used a prompt that was close to the one we both use, "If I was going to slip a page in this book and the class next door would never know it, what would it sound like?" This is now our first teaching prompt. Gayle uses a variety of texts. *These Hands* by Hope Lynne Price, *Hi, Pizza Man!* by Virginia Walter, and *No, David!* by David Shannon are a few examples of text that are easy for students to "write in their head" to create an oral text. Although Gayle uses this technique more than I, I use these texts and other repetitive texts to create books that we give as presents on our first visit to our first-grade buddies.

When we feel the kids have the hang of this, a line of text is written on a piece of chart paper, leaving out the last word. This gap is similar to cloze procedures, but this time we find many words that could fill the gap. Gayle uses a lot of books that have patterns, such as *The Tea Party* by Amy Algie. Students enjoy playing with the language of this book, creating their own texts. The text of this book is a conversation, written in speech bubbles and uses a flap design for command and response. This dialogue between a girl and her barnyard full of animals uses names and stereotypical animal noises, wonderful material for kids to play with.

While kids are innovating with these texts they are also rereading frequency words over and over. This rereading helps students learn frequent words in context, internalize language patterns, and develop automaticity for print. Students are also learning that, as writers, there are written text structures that are common, and that, as writers, we do not always need to invent ways to write our ideas. Instead, we can borrow written text structures, using language that is appropriate to convey the writer's intended message. This has become extremely important for our students as they write in a variety of genres. According to Tower (*Language Arts*, July 2005), "genres represent patterns in language use" and these language patterns are used to communicate ideas for a range of reasons. So, text innovation begins as a game. Kids play with language, molding it to fit their needs.

Differentiating Toward Fluency

Content area studies and inquiries carve out extended periods of the day. These investigations require our students to read for a variety of purposes. Students collect information, build on background knowledge, summarize information, ask questions, and synthesize what they are reading and learning. This requires text sets that include books at different reading levels. Creating text sets is a time-consuming task and at times is fruitless because there are not books at a range of levels for the topic under investigation. To combat the lack of reading material about topics, especially when introducing a topic, we read portions of the text to small groups of students.

You may think this is cheating the students by taking away the need to develop independence, or more importantly, question how this will lead to fluent reading. We have found that by the second semester, we do not need to use this teaching strategy and our students are well on their way to reading fluently.

The roots of this read-aloud thinking are grounded in the knowledge that I am not a fluent reader of all texts. Professional research data reports, technical manuals, recipes, and my son's social studies textbook are examples of texts where I have to adjust my reading rate, reread, talk out loud, and muddle my way through. To support my students when they may have this feeling, I read to them. Our social studies text or introductory content materials are the type of text that students muddle through, so these are great to use to read aloud, demonstrating fluent reading, including adjusting reading rate.

You may wonder why I don't read this material to my entire class. Pacing, time, and independence have convinced me that small-group work supports the students that need guidance, maximizing the time spent on a task, while allowing other students to be independent. The reading I am referring to is short enough that many of my students will finish their reading in seven to ten minutes and then be ready for discussion and further reading to extend their thinking. This format keeps the pace of the class moving so that a third of my students are not sitting idly and another third working at a frustration level.

Read-aloud provides many opportunities for us to promote reading and writing fluency as we provide multiple demonstrations using specific prompts. If possible we try to begin with an activity as an oral language skill and then move to a written form. These read-aloud texts are interesting to us and our students. We want to stretch their thinking, ask them to reread and learn something different while rereading. In this way, we are supporting fluency development while continually teaching the curriculum.

The lessons that follow use techniques built on read-aloud periods and other reading opportunities.

Lesson 2.1
One-Page Shared Reading

Thoughts: Shared reading of a short text is an efficient way to demonstrate fluent reading. Students begin to develop a model in their mind of what fluent reading sounds like and how to use print to read meaningfully. Since we are reading a short text and summarizing big ideas, discussion and rereading can be accomplished in a short period of time.

Planning

Think about your students' needs, deciding if this will work best as a whole-class lesson or in small-group instruction.

Prepare an overhead copy of a short text, or use a *Time for Kids* (*TFK*) *Big Picture* or big book.

You may want to listen to your students read this text independently after instruction as an assessment tool and to provide feedback.

What it looks and sounds like

We like to begin group reading experiences by setting a purpose. Since the first reading is to help students internalize the sound of fluent reading, we begin by focusing our students' attention with the following prompt. "Today we are going to read this text together. I'm going to read the first two sentences, and I want you to notice how I use my voice to match the author's words."

We then read the first two sentences and ask, "What did you notice?" While debriefing with our students, we want to guide the discussion to reading ideas and ways to sound like we were telling a story, or recounting information.

We continue the shared reading by telling our students, "I would like you to read along with me by matching your voice with mine. While you are matching your voice with mine, keep your eye on the text and think about the ideas." We read the remainder of the text in this way.

When we have finished reading the entire text, we discuss the big ideas and then ask, "What did you notice about our reading?" We again try to guide our students to the idea of reading ideas and how their voice showed their understanding of the ideas. If we had to slow down to think about an idea or word, we weave this into our conversation, often rereading that section of the text.

Lesson 2.2
Cloze Reading of Short Text

Thoughts: Many students read word by word, decoding unknown words letter by letter. To help students read ideas and use the meaning of the text with visual information to read fluently, we use a cloze reading activity. We mask a few words from a big book or text copied on an overhead transparency, or written on a chart. We prompt students to read sentences and phrases, and when they come to an unknown word, use the meaning of the text to think of the unknown word.

Planning

Assess your students' oral reading to monitor what type of visual information they use when reading an unknown word.

Prepare a big book, overhead transparency, or chart with a few words masked using a sticky note.

Be prepared to show students how to read a line of print fluently and use visual information and the meaning of the text to infer an unknown word

What it looks and sounds like

In primary grades, we found that we use this lesson at the beginning of the year with the entire class. In intermediate grades, this lesson works well with a small group of students.

"Today we are going to read _____. In this text I have masked a few words. When we come to a word that is masked, I want you to think of a word that makes sense and say that word. We will then check to see if what we said looks right. We will do this by writing on the sticky note that I have used to mask the word."

We chorally read the text. When we come to a masked word, we drop our voice out, allowing the students to predict the unknown word. We then have students write on a sticky note what they think the word will look like. We are working on helping students use the meaning of the text and structure of language to guide their prediction. The writing helps students check their prediction using visual information.

We work through a text in this manner. Masking three or four words helps students develop this idea. Keep in mind that less is more. We use this procedure until we notice that students are using this strategy in their independent reading.

Lesson 2.3
Choral Reading

Thoughts: We view our students as apprentices or novices. In using this model, it is important to demonstrate what it looks like, feels like, and sounds like to be fluent. We know that if we chorally read a text, students look at print as they internalize the feel and sound of fluent reading. We use big books, charts, and overheads of poems, stories, plays, articles, and content materials. Famous words from history like "The Gettysburg Address" or "Preamble to the Constitution" can also be used for choral reading.

Planning

Prepare an enlarged copy of a text that will work well to demonstrate how to look at print while reading fluently.

In primary grades, we like to use big books and poems on charts.

In intermediate grades, an overhead copy of a *Time For Kids* article or famous words from history grab students' attention.

What it looks and sounds like

Something we have discussed over and over again as we prepare to chorally read is how we will focus students' attention on print. We do not want to point word-by-word and interfere with fluent reading. Instead, we point to lines of print and may slide our pointer while using a big book or chart. We may use a marker or pencil on an overhead to point to punctuation as we get our students to read phrases (ideas).

We begin choral reading by prompting our students, "While I am reading this text, I would like all of you to match your voice with mine. We are going to read it like we are a choir, so let's synchronize our voices. I will point to the line we are reading. Try to make your eyes match the words you are reading."

We then read the text together. We have found that once students have internalized this reading format, students buddy read in this manner and adopt some of the language of our prompts.

When the choral reading is finished, we ask the students the self-reflection question, "What did you learn from our reading?" Students often discuss the big idea of the book first and then we discuss the use of fluency. We bring closure by asking, "How would you use what you learned about using your voice in your own reading?" We take notes of students' responses to remind students as they set goals for their independent reading.

Lesson 2.4
Highlighting Key Sentences or Phrases

Thoughts: When we sit down next to a student to monitor his or her fluent reading, the first thing we instinctively focus on is phrasing. While we listen, our ear tunes in to how students read ideas as sentences or phrases. One way we help students read ideas is by reading a text and highlighting key sentences or phrases. Then we reread the key ideas, summarizing the main idea and using supporting details.

Prepare copies of a short nonfiction text that students can mark on that is at most students' reading level. Using a *TFK* feature article or *Big Picture* is a good option.

Students need a highlighter.

Prepare an overhead copy of the short nonfiction text.

What it looks and sounds like

While we are passing out the text to use for this lesson, we prompt our students to preview the text. "When you get your text, orient yourself by looking at the title, subtitles, pictures, captions, and anything else that you notice that will help you."

We discuss what the children have discovered as they set a purpose for their reading. Then we focus the students. "Today while you are reading, I would like you to use your highlighter to highlight key sentences and phrases that help you understand the main idea(s)."

Students independently read the text. If some students can not read the text, we either read it to them or have them read with a buddy. While students are reading we circulate, noticing what is being highlighted, prompting students to read a line or two, and monitoring oral reading fluency.

When the students have finished their independent reading and highlighting, we debrief the lesson by asking, "What was the first thing you highlighted?" Students share their thinking by rereading their highlighted text, stating their rationale for highlighting and their thinking about the ideas in the text. We work through the text in this manner. This lesson promotes rereading in a purposeful setting. Even students that did not read the text independently participate. A day or two after the lesson, we ask some students to reread the text as a way to monitor the effectiveness of the lesson and their fluency development.

40

Lesson 2.5
Demonstrating Self-Monitoring (Pacing)

Thoughts: Demonstrations using read-aloud have helped our students develop inner control of many reading processes. The rich conversations and thinking that occur during read-aloud time often make our students feel like they are reading the text. Johnston (2005, p. 684) states, "Children struggling with literacy constantly turn to the teacher for feedback." We want to change these students' perceptions about themselves, teaching them how to monitor and think about their own learning. Students that are having difficulty understanding the idea of fluency and pacing learn how we use fluent reading and pacing as a means to monitor our reading and understanding. Our demonstration makes students apprentices, teaching them what fluent reading sounds and feels like and how to use it to self-monitor and set reasonable goals.

Planning

Set a block of time to read aloud to your students similar in length to students' independent reading time.

Choose a text that will challenge students to think.

What it looks and sounds like

We read aloud to our students many times each day. These read-aloud times serve different purposes such as reading to demonstrate thinking strategies, reading to understand information, appreciating poetry, and simple enjoyment, to name a few. While reading to demonstrate thinking strategies, we set a purpose for reading. The purpose helps us activate our schema to understand the text. While reading novels to our students, we have begun to share our thinking about reading pace. We have incorporated reading pace with setting a purpose.

We begin by sharing, "Today while I'm reading to you, I think I'll read _____ pages. I think I'll read this many pages because I know my reading pace. I know each day I've been reading _____ pages to you." We then write the goal on the anchor chart we use to hold our thinking.

We then read the text aloud to the students. While reading aloud, we periodically call students attention to our pacing. "Did you notice that I read through that part quickly? Did you notice how I slowed down when I was confused? My prediction wasn't right. Did you notice how I slowed down because that word was unfamiliar? Did you notice that I reread that section? I reread because I wanted to figure out the meaning of _____."

41

When we are finished with the read-aloud for the day, we reflect on our pacing goal. "I didn't meet my goal today. Tomorrow I may need to read a bit faster and maybe I should read on instead of rereading. Maybe I'm not predicting what will come next and that is slowing me down. I could lower my goal." We discuss each option, put together a plan for the next day's read-aloud, and use it the next day.

Lesson 2.6
Read the Punctuation: Ending Punctuation

Thoughts: Fluent readers' oral reading demonstrates their understanding of the text. End punctuation (period, question mark, and exclamation point) helps the reader interpret the meaning of the text. Helping students read end punctuation will guide students' fluent reading.

Planning

Choose a big book that can serve as an example of how an author has used ending punctuation. You can use a variety of fiction, nonfiction, and poetry.

Set a time for students to read and note how authors are using ending punctuation.

Prepare a chart to record examples of ending punctuation being used in a variety of ways.

What it looks and sounds like

We want our students to read to the end of each idea. Fluent readers use their voice as a tool to interpret the meaning of a text while reading orally. We have discovered that many of our students read through end punctuation, misunderstanding what they have read. Students blend ideas from the end of one sentence with the next. When the ideas don't match, students are confused. Many students realize they are confused but either do not know why they are lost or do not have self-repair strategies.

To help our students understand why they need to pause at the end of a sentence, we focus on end punctuation. The lesson begins with the students listening to oral reading of a short text. A picture book like *Halloween* by Jerry Seinfeld works well because it uses a variety of end punctuation and the text sounds like his monologue. Robert Munsch's books also work well since his stories were rehearsed as oral stories.

While students are listening we ask them, "Listen to how I use my voice to make the words come to life. Listen to when I stop before going on to the next idea. While I read, think about what type of end punctuation the author used." Then read the story, allowing the students to hear how you use end punctuation as a tool to guide your oral reading interpretation and to separate ideas.

After demonstrating your use of end punctuation, have students read texts you have selected, noticing and noting end punctuation. Chart the students' discoveries. Reread the chart, reflecting on how the examples help your oral reading and interpretation. **Revisit the chart periodically to reinforce fluent reading.**

43

Lesson 2.7
Read the Punctuation: Internal Punctuation

Thoughts: Fluent readers read ideas. These ideas are embedded in words, phrases, and clauses within simple, compound, and complex sentences. Reading and understanding internal punctuation marks helps readers read ideas fluently. We help students understand how authors use internal punctuation as a tool to craft their ideas. When we think of internal punctuation, we talk with our students about commas, quotation marks, parentheses, semicolons, and colons.

Planning

Select a big book that can serve as an example of how an author has used internal punctuation. You can use a variety of fiction, nonfiction, and poetry.

Set a time for students to read and note how authors are using internal punctuation.

Prepare a chart to record examples of internal punctuation being used in a variety of ways.

What it looks and sounds like

We have found that many of our students think that commas are primarily used to list ideas in a series. This is a good place to begin. Find a big book or enlarge a short text that illustrates comma use. Prior to reading the text to your students, prompt them to listen to your reading, "While I'm reading, listen to how I use the punctuation to guide my voice."

Read the text to your students, adjusting your voice so that your students will recognize how you adjusted your phrasing when you came to the comma. When you have read the entire text, ask, "What did you notice about my reading?" Guide your students to discuss why you adjusted your voice.

Then read another passage to your students that has commas used to separate clauses. Ask your students, "How was the comma used in this text? What did I do with my voice to read the passage?" Discuss your phrasing.

Ask your students to read the books you have gathered, noticing how commas are used. Give your students adequate time to read, reread, and discuss commas. Record your students' discoveries on a chart. Reread these lines, using fluent phrasing. Challenge your students to find more examples to add to this chart. Students add to this chart over the course of the year as they encounter commas used in a variety of ways. Students internalize comma use, using them to read fluently and as a tool in their writing.

We go through similar steps for other internal punctuation.

Lesson 2.8
Text Innovation

Thoughts: Innovating from a text is borrowing or learning from a mentor text. No matter which title we give it, it helps students develop fluency because they are reading and rereading a text and thinking about how an author has put their idea down on paper. The rereading helps the students read and internalize story grammars. It supports students' fluent writing because it provides a model for writing their own ideas. It prevents students from thinking "I don't know how to say that."

Planning

Be prepared with an example of how you innovated from a mentor text.

Find a text that will serve as a good example of writing for your students.

In primary grades, you could use a big book to show students how to move from the author's words to their own ideas.

Use chart paper to record innovations.

What it looks and sounds like

We want our students to learn to write from real authors. One of the ways we have helped our students develop writing voices is by studying authors. Robert Munsch, Eric Carle, Cynthia Rylant, Eve Bunting, Karen Hesse, Ralph Fletcher, and many other children's authors help our students learn how to craft their thinking.

We show students how to innovate by using a text they are familiar with from read-aloud or shared reading of a big book. We begin by rereading the part we will use as a model for writing (i.e., Eric Carle's beginning, "In the light of the moon . . ."). We like to write the line we are going to use on the chart so that students can see how we innovated or changed words to match our writing need. Then we think out loud, telling the students what we like about the line of text and how we may change it to meet our writing need. In intermediate grades, nonfiction texts work well.

We then take the idea and "write in the air." Writing in the air is just orally rehearsing the idea that will be put on paper. After repeating the line a few times, we write it on the chart paper underneath the line from the text that was used for borrowing.

We then reflect with students by asking, "What did you notice I did?" We use this question to discuss places the text was changed and why.

45

We finish by asking students to use the line from the text to craft a line together, and then use shared writing to record the line. We try to write two or three lines together. We bring closure by asking, "Where and how could you use this strategy?"

REREADING

3

"There are several formats for repeated reading. Most involve text that is easy to understand and provides an appropriate balance of success and challenge in word recognition."

Jo Worthy, Karen Broaddus, and Gay Ivey, *Pathways to Independence,* 2001

At the beginning of the year, John, a first-grader, stated that his reading goal was to sound like Mrs. Brand and his mother when he read. John had been caught in the spell of story language at home and school. He realized the powerful effect he could have while reading, and he wanted this power. One morning Gayle received a note from John's mother asking her to persuade John to reread books he was bringing home. John felt that rereading was a waste of his time, since he'd read the book already.

Gayle talked with her class and John about the importance of doing something over and over so that they get good at it. Gayle used the example of Michael Jordan; even though he was the best basketball player in the NBA, he still practiced his dribbling and shooting each day. He even hired a coach to help him practice. John took this to heart and started rereading books, at home and in school, surprising himself with how fluently he could read familiar books in front of his classmates. Soon he did sound like Mrs. Brand and his mom when he read aloud.

Repeated reading is one of the recommendations from the National Reading Panel and researchers (Samuels, Allington, Rasinski, and others) that calls for oral and silent rereading to be used as an instructional tool to build fluency. Repeated reading builds written language patterns in students' heads. Students are developing knowledge of common written language patterns as they occur in texts they read and then reread. This written language background is then used by the reader to anticipate phrases and words while they are reading. Goodman (1970) reminds us that in both oral and written language we rely on an anticipatory set, predicting what will come next, anticipating oral language utterances or which written word will come next. Clay (1991) has labeled this system as a feed-forward mechanism, a critical feature of a fluent reader's reading process. Repeated reading also builds a reading sight vocabulary as students reread frequent words and phrases in familiar, authentic texts.

We also realize that we are not going to be fluent with a skill or strategy after one exposure—practice makes perfect. By repeating the task (reading) and using skills and strategies, the reader begins the process of developing fluency. As learners become fluent, they can use this knowledge base to learn more complex skills. Fluid performers can divide their attention toward specific aspects of a skill or strategy. While rereading, the reader has background knowledge of the main idea so attention can be directed toward new learning, either in context or out of context. This supports the growth of automatic word recognition skills because readers can divide their attention, using their understanding of the text and structure of the passage while closely examining a word. They can notice syllables, letter clusters, and letters or use the sub-word to learn how words work. Teaching word-solving skills or demonstrating fluent reading is easily reinforced during rereading.

Ideally students reread texts that are considered easy and read with an accuracy rate of ninety-five percent. We know that as students reread short texts, content material, poems, and charts they may not read at ninety-five percent accuracy. To support our learners, we have found shared reading or choral reading to be effective rereading instructional strategies. A goal is for students to read and reread texts that provide a few opportunities to decode words, internalize sight words and decoding strategies, and become automatic, fluent readers of novel texts.

Why Do We Reread?

To prepare for rereading demonstrations, Gayle and I think about the reasons we revisit texts in our reading lives. While demonstrating the value of rereading, we want to talk to our students about the importance of rereading in helping us understand what we are reading. One way we demonstrate rereading is by bringing in a text (book, magazine, memo, our own writing) that confused us. We introduce the demonstration by telling our students where we were confused and what our thinking was that made us stop, reread, and think about the confusing part. Students find out that we sometimes misread punctuation, mispronounce words, read too fast, or may not think clearly about our reading.

We also talk about our professional reading. Depending upon our purpose, we reread parts of a text many times. We talk about rereading texts we will use in writing projects or the books we refer to often to help us become more effective teachers. We also read recipes and directions many times—before, during, and after the project. We may reread books or poems as preparation for class, or before talking with each other or a colleague about an intriguing idea. Over the course of the year, we talk about and demonstrate the importance of rereading to help us understand and think more deeply about what we are reading.

We ask kids to reread a variety of texts every day. These texts are typically short, interesting to our students, and lead to thoughtful conversations. We want rereading to be purposeful, similar to our real-world examples. Texts that we typically use for rereading are:

- Excerpts from *Time for Kids* and other news magazines written for children

- Poems

- Picture books

- Books in baskets

- Songs

- Math story problems

- Students' writing

- Mentor texts in writing genre study

- Charts

- Shared and interactive writing pieces

- Word walls

Rereading to Start the School Day

Time is an issue in my classroom, no matter how efficient I am. The first few minutes are used for my students to read a short text (reading on demand). This text often sets the tone for the day, propelling our thinking about a content inquiry, newsworthy event, or something that I know will interest my students. These texts are typically short, can be read quickly (five–ten minutes), and

---

Rereading Morning Message Prompts

Reread your *Time For Kids* article, thinking about why the article was called, _____. Highlight words, phrases, and sentences that make you think this way. Be ready to discuss your thinking.

Reread pages _____ from your social studies textbook. While you are rereading this section, find key words and ideas that will help you answer the focus question.

Reread a text from _____ text set. While rereading from the text set find a (lead/concluding) (sentence/paragraph) that you would like to write like. Copy this into the love of language section of your word study notebook. Then write your own _____, using this mentor text.

Reread the poem, _____, thinking about this idea, _____. Highlight words, phrases, and lines that make you think this way. Be ready to discuss your thinking.

Find a poem to bring alive. Once you have found a poem, reread it, paying attention to the rhythm of words, flow of lines, and punctuation. Once you have reread it a few times, you may want to share with a buddy.

Reread the _____ anchor chart. Make sure it makes sense and says what we have discussed.

Reread the word wall. Find a word you want to use in your writing. Use this word in a new piece of writing or in previous work in your writing notebook. Be ready to share your writing.

Reread the words and phrases on the wall. Find words or phrases that you think we should take down. Be ready to explain why you think the word or phrase should come down.

Figure 3.1 Rereading Morning Message Prompts

invite students to think about the world and discuss what they have learned from the text. The discussion leads students to reread the article to show the sources of their thinking. This purposeful rereading, thinking, and discussion are learned behaviors that take time, practice, and multiple opportunities to become a habit of mind.

Students in my class have learned the routine of entering the classroom, unpacking book bags, greeting classmates, and reading a personal, crafted message on the board that sets the agenda for the first ten or fifteen minutes of the day. Staggered student arrival has been typical no matter where I have taught—an urban setting or the suburbs. Whether teaching in primary grades or intermediate, I try to maximize learning time. Reading on demand, buddy reading, and rereading a variety of texts help me maximize learning by using time efficiently. While students are reading, I can move around the room, coaching, observing, noting student behavior, and preparing for the follow-up discussion and lesson.

At the beginning of the year while students are learning how to accomplish this morning reading activity, they all read the same text and I like to debrief the reading session using an enlarged copy of the reading passage on the overhead. I begin by asking, "What were the challenges with this morning's reading?" I have adopted this to be my standard, routine question, because it is important for students to internalize that we all have challenges. These challenges can range from classroom management issues (noise level, off-task behaviors) to challenging words in the text, or, most importantly, understanding what this text is saying.

When I ask this question at the beginning of the year, silence is a natural response, but I don't allow this silence to frustrate me. Instead, I use demonstration as a tool, showing students an area of the text that confused me and caused me to reread it and think about the idea and why it was written in this manner. Once the kids get the hang of this routine and are liberated to talk about challenges, our conversation focuses on rereading to untangle confusions and focus on big ideas.

"What were the challenges with this morning's reading?" My typical morning greeting interrupts my students' chatter while they transition from reading to forming a cluster for discussion in our meeting area. They have just finished an initial reading and buddy talk about "The Big Chill" (from *Write Time for Kids*). This article has presented ways winter weather affects life in Alaska. The students are very interested in school-related issues, school closing, and recess.

"I think it would be challenging living in Anchorage, because school rarely closes," Alex sarcastically responds. Brady adds, "It's all the inside recess that I couldn't take."

The kids begin to reread a paragraph without my prompting:

> *Alaskans take bad weather in stride. Schools hardly ever close just because it's cold. Only when the temperature dips to −20F are students excused from outdoor recess.*

Dylan breaks in, "I couldn't take that cold in stride." Jenna inquires, "What does it mean, 'Alaskans take bad weather in stride'?"

Paxson answers, "I think it means you just go along with it. You know, as things come up you go along with it. After I read the sentence '*Cars won't start, so people bring car batteries inside for the night*' I went back and reread that sentence a couple times, and that's how I knew what it meant. That is an example of taking the cold in stride."

The conversation continues, focused on taking the cold weather in stride. Students find many examples of this idea by rereading and sharing some interesting language used in the article. My students have begun to learn the importance of rereading as they think deeply about their reading and find supporting details and important vocabulary.

My fifth-graders are learning from their rereading and learning how to read. I ask my students to read and reread a common text as a springboard into content learning or to teach a reading strategy. The reading, rereading, and discussion often lay the groundwork for further reading, questions, and exploration along a content strand. Lattimer (2003, p. 17) comments, "And as a teacher, I need texts that will allow me to create short, focused lessons that communicate ideas succinctly." Teaching a reading strategy aids students as they independently read from content material. Rereading as a reading strategy is important to all of us.

Gayle's day begins with students coming in during a fifteen-minute window stretching from the first latch-key student to the last student who walks to school. Students enter, check in for lunch, empty their book bags, hang up their belongings, stop to share a note or news about their evening or morning, and then go to find their seats. Their seats change daily because Gayle deals out their name cards each morning. Students sit with a variety of their peers, depending on the focus for the day. This promotes a stronger sense of community because tablemates change daily. It also allows students to interact in a variety of roles because they are not cast into the same grouping patterns.

As they settle into their seats for the day, kids shuffle through the book basket that is placed in the middle of their table. They choose a book to begin to read. This buddy reading time is when students are reading, sharing, discussing, comparing, and thinking with each other about books. The books in the baskets are familiar. Songs, read-aloud texts, multiple copies of shared reading texts, poems, and *Time for Kids* magazines are all placed in book baskets. Books placed in baskets include various levels, genres, and styles. The books are changed at the beginning of each month, and the baskets are randomly put at tables each morning. This allows students to develop phrasing and fluency with known and new texts and the time to assist and share with one another about books. They gain access to more books than they might if the books were only chosen for each child's level of reading, and it helps them develop their abilities to discuss, share, and question in relation to books.

Selecting books for baskets is a thoughtful process. The baskets each have twenty to thirty books in them and are changed each month. Some titles are added to the baskets during the month. The selection of texts include books by the author the class is studying that month, magazines of various levels (*Spider, Ladybug, Your Backyard, Zoo Books*), poetry, nonfiction (of varying difficulty and usually connected to the content students are studying that month), holiday books, short chapter books, picture books, math books, leveled books (PM Readers, Wright Group, KEEP books, etc.), song books, and student writing (once it has been published and shared with the class). Each table has a different basket of books. The baskets have some of the same titles, typically songs, patterned texts, extra *Time for Kids* magazines, and favorites with multiple copies. The baskets rotate from table to table so that students are exposed to a wide variety of reading material. The baskets are also available during reading workshop, allowing students to reread titles and examine the texts more closely.

Gayle circulates during this time; her clipboard has a grid sheet with a box for each student. Her role is to observe student behaviors. She monitors the student's book choice, the interaction with the book, and strategies the student may exhibit when encountering a new or difficult word, phrase, or idea. Gayle also notes if students are reading orally, whispering, lip reading, or reading silently. She may ask a student to read orally so that she can document phrasing, pacing, and fluency. These notes are records she uses to plan individual, small-group, and whole-class instruction.

Gayle's students reread familiar texts. They choose what texts they want to reread from the basket that is placed at their table. Gayle feels that students need to read and reread a variety of texts and genres as they become fluent

•Week of Feb 6th - 10th

Reading Workshop

Abbey	Alya (2/8) Junie B. Jones · Book is too difficult, we decide she should choose a different book	Alyssa	Aspen (2/10) When I was Young in the Mountains • revisiting yesterday's read aloud • enjoys repetition • using phrasing	Audrey
Austin (2/6) The Lady with the Alligator Purse (song) • enjoys song books- sings out loud	Bailey	Carter	Elaina	Ellie (2/7) Try to Be a Brave Girl Sarah (F) • whisper reads book 3 times
Grant (2/6) Whales (nonfiction) • recording interesting facts while reading into observation log	Hannah	Jacob (2/8) Lion and the Mouse • lip reading while pointing at words	John (2/6) Mortimer • reads pattern using a voice like mine from read aloud	Jordan (2/9) Horrible Harry • "Lost" in book- reading silently • Hard to get her attention
Kara	Lexi	Michael (2/9) Zoobook magazine • interested in text • studying pictures, trying to read captions • Tommy helps him	Naomi (2/7) • Reads with Stephanie • Comparing Robert munsch books	Niko
Seth	Stephanie (2/7) • Reading with Naomi • Comparing Robert munsch books	Tommy (2/9) Zoobook magazine • helping michael to read captions		

Figure 3.2 Gayle's Anecdotal Notes

readers. Rereading on demand for Gayle supports this belief, exposing her students to a variety of texts and allowing them to choose what they will read. They are learning from their rereading and learning to read. Gayle can use the child's rereading of a familiar text to teach a specific skill or strategy and help the student be a bit more independent the rest of the day.

Gayle brings her class together by asking the same question as I do, "What were the challenges with this morning's reading?" Tommy comments, "While I was reading this morning some of the words just rolled off my tongue, but other words were hard." Hannah adds, "The more we read the same books, the more we sound like you, Mrs. Brand." Gayle asks Tommy what he did when some of the words were hard. "I reread the sentence and thought about what was going on in the book" is Tommy's response. Gayle capitalizes on this teachable moment by asking Tommy to show the class how this strategy helped him. Tommy retrieves *Simple Machines* by L. Schaefer. He turns to page 8, showing how he reread the sentence after looking at the picture and caption. Gayle also has one or two students read aloud an interesting idea or an enjoyable part of a text.

Rereading Read-Aloud Books and Charts

While reading aloud fiction, nonfiction, or poetry, we also reread. We reread lines or words that grab our attention. These words or lines have made us think more deeply about the text. I read aloud poems twice prior to discussion, a ritual I've established with my students. We also revisit anchor charts and words and phrases on our word walls. When we are rereading, kids are learning about written language, phrases, frequency of words and language patterns, how writers put together words to express ideas, and what fluent reading sounds like. We are also helping kids learn about the melody of oral reading, timing, phrasing, expression, intonation, and where to place stress.

While students transition from one activity to the next, we reread so that students do not sit idly, waiting for classmates. It is amazing how quickly and quietly Gayle's kids clean up and then join in the rereading of familiar texts. It serves as a great time-management tool for transitions. It keeps the pace of the classroom humming along. Rereading books that have refrains like *The Three Billy Goats Gruff; No, David!; The Recess Queen;* or *Mortimer* helps students internalize language patterns and enjoy language and rereading. It quickly brings stragglers together with the rest of the class. Shared reading materials and poetry also help during transition times.

We have both developed the habit of keeping charts that include language from read-aloud books, poetry, and songs. Gayle has charts with refrains on them that her students flip to and recite while rereading. Students not only develop an ear for what fluent reading sounds like, but develop automaticity with print and learn how grammar guides their phrasing. Both of us also write poems on charts and keep overhead copies so that as we reread and reexamine these texts, students can listen and see the text as they participate in choral and shared reading.

My students keep a word wall of interesting lines from read-aloud texts. These lines or passages are revisited when students reread them orally and silently while they think about the meaning of the line, why the author may have used it, and why it is important to understand the text. The word wall may also include exemplars that students use as mentor texts for their writing. The power in these lines is that the group has made the decision about what will go up on the chart or wall, why it is important to them, and how it will extend their thinking and develop fluency as both readers and writers.

55

Rereading Charts and Word Walls

- Students reread anchor charts as a tool for their content writing.
- Students reread anchor charts as directions for accomplishing a task.
- Students reread shared writing and interactive writing charts to revise and edit.
- Students reread anchor charts to ensure that it accurately describes an activity.
- Students reread words or phrases on the word walls as mentor texts or as seed ideas.
- Students reread word walls to monitor and self-correct their spelling.

Figure 3.3 Rereading Charts and Word Walls

Bringing Poetry to Life

Purposeful rereading is a cornerstone belief that drives our fluency instruction; it helps students value the purpose behind the task. We both enjoy poetry, realizing that it is meant to be read orally. The best way to capture the cadence, rhythm, and flow of poetry is to repeatedly read it orally, thinking about bringing the words to life. We incorporate poetry reading into our daily routine.

"Poetry 180" is Billy Collins' poem-a-day program for schools (www. loc.gov/poetry/180/). It is an instructional tool that we use to read, reread, discuss, and think about poetry. We structure this activity to read poems twice before discussing them. The first reading allows the students to tune their ear, listening to the flow of language, thinking about what the poem might mean. The second time through, students are anticipating words, thinking about ideas within phrases, clarifying what they did not understand during the first reading. Once our students are comfortable with this format, we copy the poem on a chart, use the overhead projector to show students how the poem is formatted, or make a copy of the poem for all our students to read along.

We discuss the poem, prompting students to recall or reread words, phrases, or lines that have shaped their thinking. After rereading a specific section from the poem, a typical response is, "I like how the poet painted a picture with the words." When noting the author's use of punctuation and how it guided the oral reading and is connected to the meaning of the poem, a student often says, "I like how the poet used punctuation to make my voice read it." Having a copy of the poem in front of the students encourages them to reread and think about the ideas and phrases in the poem, similar to our demonstrations. Copied poems are kept in poetry folders.

We also have students share their poetry discoveries with their classmates. We call this poetry share "Bringing Poetry to Life." The title of the activity suggests to the children the purpose for their rereading. Students look through our classroom poetry collections, individually, in pairs, or as a small group. While they are searching for a poem to read to their classmates, we ask them to find a poem that is calling to be read aloud. At times this becomes a noisy ten or fifteen minutes as students find poems. They read them to classmates and get their tongues tied as they try to use the meaning of the poem, punctuation, and phrases to guide their oral reading.

Students then come together with their discovered poems and perform them for their classmates. While students are listening to their peers perform, they are thinking about the meaning of the poem, how the poem sounds orally, and if they would recite that poem in the same way. Students start to internalize the self-monitoring questions: "Does that sound right?" "Does that sound like talk?" "Does the reading flow?" These are questions we have been using with our students and which they then use with each other.

On Tuesdays, our students take their poetry folders home. Students reread favorite poems that they have collected in their poetry folder. The kids add illustrations or borders to poems, creating pictures that they feel represent ideas expressed in the poems. Our students may also be asked to highlight words that pop out, are unusual, or are used frequently. They may also highlight a phrase, sentence, or stanza and use this as a mentor text, playing with a seed idea that will be used to write their own poem. What is important to us is that our students are rereading collected materials. They are learning to bring the words and ideas to life by using their voices. We are extending this work beyond the classroom walls, attempting to create fluent habits for our learners.

Our students also write, reread, and perform their own poetry. We ask students to find mentor poems that help shape their understanding of poetry and guide their own writing. Our students develop reading fluency by rereading mentor poems, paying attention to the rhythm, rhyme, cadence, phrases, stanzas, and format of these poems. Students reading mentor poems first notice the author's craft and its intent. Slowing the pace of their reading, students ask themselves, "What is the poet doing?" "Why is the author using this crafting technique?" This causes the students to reread the text, noting sentence length, grammar, and punctuation and building a storehouse of oral and written language.

When our students are crafting poems, they are rereading their own work to themselves or with a buddy, monitoring the rhythm and flow of their words, practicing fluent reading, and creating meaningful poems. Students periodically perform their poetry informally for classmates and select school personnel. Once or twice a year we invite friends and family for a poetry reading.

Series Text

Students not only revisit and reread the same text but they also read books from a series. Books from a series support transitional and fluent readers' fluency in ways similar to patterned texts for emergent and early readers. Pattern texts are predictable. Emergent readers build fluency by reading repetitive patterned texts which usually only change a word or two each page. Emerging readers use picture cues and a beginning letter to read an unknown word. Students memorize these texts from multiple readings, internalizing frequent written phrases. Early readers read texts that use familiar language patterns and repeating sentences and phrases. Students continue to build a sight vocabulary while reading and rereading these texts. Students also internalize more sophisticated written phrases and sentences. Early readers often encounter the same character in multiple stories and learn from their reading how characters act and talk. They use this background knowledge as they encounter the character in a variety of different settings and plots.

Series books provide students with similar background knowledge. Students learn how a character acts, talks, and reacts while reading a series of texts. Students become comfortable with a writer's style, know the setting and how to follow the plot structure. Students use this background knowledge to read fluently. Many of my friends are not Tom Clancy fans because they don't feel comfortable with his writing style. I enjoy his writing style, have a familiarity with his characters, and enjoy his winding plots. So these books are easy for me to read, even in public places like the noisy pool or busy airport.

Students who are having difficulty with fluency enjoy reading series books. Aaron liked reading the *Henry and Mudge* books by Cynthia Rylant once he read the first text, understanding the relationship between Henry and his dog Mudge. He used his understanding of one series as he read another, *Frog and Toad* by Arnold Lobel. Connecting what he knew about series texts led him to start reading the *Cam Jansen* series by David Adler. He knew the first chapter would introduce him to Cam's photographic memory and why she was called Cam. Reading series text not only helps students read fluently, but knowing about the plot structure also helps them understand when to adjust their reading rate. Two of my at-risk students, Jenna and Jessica, chose to read titles from series. They worked their way through the series of *ABC Mysteries* by Ron Roy, *The Magic Tree House* by Mary Pope Osborne and *Yang* by Lensey Namioka. They ended the school year reading *Shiloh* by Phyllis Reynold Naylor, with plans to finish the series during the summer.

Series Text Support

- A character's personality, speech patterns, and actions make them familiar and help when predicting how the character will act in a new situation.
- The author's writing style and vocabulary are familiar.
- Repeated phrases and themes make them familiar.
- Plot structures are familiar, making the text predictable.
- The setting is familiar so readers do not have to orient themselves to this feature.
- The lengths of the text are similar so that readers know how to pace themselves through the text.

Figure 3.4 Series Text Support

Students not only read from series, they also read books by the same author. Roald Dahl and Jerry Spinelli are favorite authors that explore similar ideas in their text, but through the exploits of other characters. Students connect one story to the other using background knowledge of the writer's style. Students read the texts fluently, adjusting the reading rate by knowing how these familiar authors craft stories. Students read fluently not only from series texts and familiar authors, but also about familiar topics.

Students also listen to and read books by authors during an author study. Gayle's students study Kevin Henkes, Eric Carle, and Robert Munsch, to name a few. The students learn about Robert Munsch using repetitive phrases. Eric Carle has a series of books that Gayle's students have labeled, "The Very." Students reread these books for pleasure, learning about the writing craft as they learn to be fluent readers that read like fluent writers.

We use text sets of books during content area studies. These text sets are put together around a common theme and include texts at multiple reading levels. While students are building background knowledge, they may read easier texts. We also read snippets from these texts. We introduce our students to important ideas and text structures and develop vocabulary. Gayle's primary-age students not only like to reread these books in class, but also take them home to read with their parents. Students reread the same idea in more challenging books as they continue to learn and read during a content study. Their rereading helps them develop fluency, not only in this collection of books, but in the genre of nonfiction. Students learn how to adjust their reading pace as they read and reread nonfiction texts for a variety of purposes during a content area study.

Author Text Support

- The author's writing style and vocabulary are familiar.
- The author uses similar settings and characters.
- The author writes about similar themes.
- The author uses a similar writing style and voice.
- The author repeats favorite words and phrases.
- The reader connects with the author.

Figure 3.5 Author Text Support

Our students have developed the habit of rereading texts, passages, sentences, and words for a variety of purposes. We continuously demonstrate the variety of purposes for rereading texts. Rereading becomes a natural part of reading and writing instruction over the course of the year. Students like John and Aaron have benefited from purposeful oral rereading as they have worked towards becoming fluent readers. We know that large-group instruction is only one instructional setting that supports students' fluency awareness and development. We use the seeds developed in large-group instruction to work on fluency and automaticity with words in small groups. These small-group settings allow us to continue guiding students by using feedback to improve their reading and writing fluency.

The lessons that follow build on rereading strategies to help develop fluency.

Lesson 3.1
Bringing Poetry to Life

Thoughts: When a poem excites us, we will reread it to understand it. We will also reread the poem to bring it to life for others. Having students reread poems before bringing them to life for their classmates is an easy way to prompt students to purposefully reread a text. Primary-age students also reread (sing) songs that are part of their poetry folder or song books included in book baskets.

Planning

Be prepared with your own favorite poem to demonstrate how to bring a poem to life.

Collect a variety of poetry collections.

Set a time for students to bring poetry to life and receive feedback.

What it looks and sounds like

Students need to have an authentic purpose for rereading texts. One of those purposes is performance. Bringing poetry to life helps students read and reread texts (poems) and think about meaning and how to use their voices to show their understanding. Primary-age students may bring songs to life with movement.

We'll read aloud one of our favorite poems from *Turtle in July* by Marilyn Singer. While orally reading the poem, we'll ask students, "How did my voice help you understand the poem?" The prompt is designed to focus students on thinking about how fluent reading helped them understand the poem. This oral reading is designed to help students begin to understand the importance of reading ideas, emphasizing key words, speeding up and slowing down—bringing the poem to life.

Then we'll ask students to work with a buddy to find a poem they can bring to life. While students are orally sharing, the group monitors fluent reading using the question, "How did my voice help you understand the poem?" The group provides feedback related to this question.

Lesson 3.2
Charting Challenges in Reading

Thoughts: An anchor chart is a tool that we use to hold thinking on and focus classroom conversations. We chart our reading challenges so that students realize that we all have similar challenges and strategies that help us. We reread these anchor charts, first for clarity and then to think how they help us read strategically.

Planning

Prior to charting challenges, spend a week or two discussing reading challenges and how to strategically work through those confusions.

Prepare blank chart paper.

What it looks and sounds like

Before we chart reading challenges we use read-aloud, shared reading, small-group reading, and conferences to discuss reading challenges and strategies for untangling these confusions. When we pull our class together to create an anchor chart, it is a tool to hold our thinking so we can reflect and use charted strategies.

We begin creating our anchor chart by asking, "What are your challenges while reading?" Students' responses typically address decoding, vocabulary, fluency, and comprehension challenges. The initial responses are a great way to monitor what your students understand from your instruction. We prompt our students to extend their thinking by probing, "What strategies do you use to help yourself when your reading is challenging?"

This helps us refocus the conversation as we begin to categorize students' confusions into categories such as decoding, vocabulary, fluency, and comprehension. While creating this anchor chart, we work on oral language fluency by asking students to state the confusion and strategy clearly. We then write statements on the chart, reread them and, if necessary, revise them. This helps students read ideas in meaningful chunks and consider the big idea.

Creating these charts may take a couple of days. Students' attention may wane after fifteen minutes. The initial charts may be messy. Recopy the messy chart, asking your students to reread it and make sure this is what they wanted to say. Revisit these charts prior to independent reading and small-group work to guide students' reading.

Lesson 3.3
Pondering Poetry

Thoughts: When preparing to read a poem to my class we usually read it a few times. While reading the poem, we consider how to read the ideas. We use the lines, words, punctuation, and stanzas as clues while rehearsing for poetry reading. Pondering while rereading is a strategy we want my students to use as they rehearse for reading aloud, but more importantly while they are reading a novel text.

Planning

Prepare an enlarged poem or overhead copy of poem.

Select a poem for students to practice. "Deer Mouse" from *Turtle in July* by M. Singer is a favorite for primary- and intermediate-grade students.

What it looks and sounds like

While reading poems aloud to our students, we have adopted the practice of reading it twice. Students typically tune in during the first reading and begin to explore the poet's message during the second reading. Borrowing from two-read practice, we have adapted our teaching to invite students to notice our use of voice as they interpret meaning.

To help students understand how to ponder and reflect on how to use their voices as a way to give the poem meaning, we read the poem line by line. Since the students are looking at an enlarged version of the poem or their own personal copy, we say, "That didn't sound right. The way my voice sounded didn't make sense. I missed something."

Before rereading we tell our students, "This time when I read _____, I'm going to keep an eye on the punctuation. I'm going to let it help me breathe and think while I read." We reread the poem more fluently and then ask, "What did you notice?"

We debrief the lesson, discussing how we used punctuation to make the poem make sense. Our discussion includes how ideas are grouped together. We then ask the students, "What have you learned that can be used when you read?"

Students then read poems in groups, practicing and monitoring their fluent reading. Students seem to get the hang of it quickly but benefit from this lesson periodically on more challenging poems.

Lesson 3.4
Revisiting Anchor Charts

Thoughts: Anchor charts hold a prominent place on our classroom walls. These charts anchor thinking, helping our students understand the how and why of reading or writing strategies. Rereading these charts is a purposeful rereading activity. We reread these charts to ensure they capture thinking or as a reminder of how and why to use a literacy strategy.

Planning

Prepare anchor charts.

Demonstrate rereading by setting a purpose for revisiting an anchor chart.

Help students understand the purpose for rereading an anchor chart.

What it looks and sounds like

We begin guiding students' rereading of anchor charts after we have crafted our first anchor chart. I make the first anchor chart for word study after a week of word observations. "This morning I am going to read you a Word Observation anchor chart. While I am reading it out loud, I want you to read along with me. While we are reading together, we can make sure this chart states how we do Word Observation. The writing should be clear so that someone that has never done Word Observation could use this chart to help them do it without any other explanation."

While rereading the Word Observation chart or any other anchor chart, students learn how to read ideas fluently. They also learn the importance of rereading their own writing and monitoring meaning.

Lesson 3.5
Revisiting Word Walls

Thoughts: Hanging words, phrases, sentences, and ideas on classroom walls is not a novel idea. Our word walls have high frequency and frequently misspelled words. Asking students to read these words and word connection charts helps them develop automaticity, a critical part of fluent reading.

Planning

Construct a word wall and/or Making Connections charts.

Assess students' reading, noting their fluency with high frequency words.

Determine students that need to read and reread words automatically.

What it looks and sounds like

Reading high frequency words and words that have the same rime pattern as high frequency words helps students read fluently. Some students do not read high frequency words automatically. To build up our students' automatic reading of high frequency words, we spend three to five minutes reading our word wall and Making Connections charts.

Small-group instruction works best while reading from the word wall. When we pull a group of students, we tell them, "We are going to read the words from the word wall. I want you to read them as quickly as possible while I point to them. I'm going to time how long it takes us to read these words." We read the words from the wall each day, trying to improve our time and developing automaticity. We do not point to the words in the same order each day.

Once the students have caught on to the flow of this sight-reading activity, we include the Making Connections charts to our reading.

When the students are fluent and flexible when reading sight words and Making Connections charts, we then use the prompt, "Tell me a connected word," when pointing to a word wall word.

Lesson 3.6
Picture Walk

Thoughts: We have developed the habit of previewing texts before reading them. A guided picture walk is an opportunity to help students develop this habit. The picture walk helps students build schema for the text, which supports their fluent reading.

Planning

Be prepared to use an enlarged text or a big book to demonstrate what a picture walk looks and sounds like.

Select a group of students that are challenged to read fluently.

Select a text or book that students will read with about 95 percent accuracy.

What it looks and sounds like

Students often preview a text prior to reading it. This previewing helps readers build schema for the text they are going to read. While previewing a text, we usually use new vocabulary so students can hear unfamiliar terms and may ask students to look at pictures or captions, as a means for understanding how to search for meaning.

"Today we are going to read _____ by _____" This is how we help students tune into a picture walk. "Today we are going to look at the text and think about the big ideas we may read about in the text."

We look through the text, noticing text features (nonfiction), or use the pictures in a narrative text to think about the plot of the story.

We then ask students to read the text independently. While the students are reading the text independently, we monitor their fluency by sitting next to them and listening to their oral reading.

When the students have finished reading the text, we bring them together, often having them revisit challenges while reading interesting parts.

SHORT BURSTS FOR BUILDING STAMINA

4

I can still remember my first experience in organized sports, freshman basketball. We had a wonderful coach, Mr. Orr, who left a lasting impression on my thinking and teaching. Coach Orr had an uncanny ability to motivate us and get the team to overachieve by demonstrating basic skills (shooting, dribbling, and passing). He provided constant feedback that was specific, so that we could continue to build skills and develop as team players. Coach Orr expected our team to achieve at a high level, and we did. Our successes were celebrated, no matter how small, which brought us together as a team and motivated us to work harder.

The most memorable lessons were the drills to build stamina; "killers" we fondly named them. We would begin and end practice with forty-eight ticks on the scoreboard clock. The team had to complete a series of sprints in this amount of time or challenge ourselves again. These sprints were designed to help us build stamina, developing endurance for our ultimate test, game day. Thinking back now, practice moved at a brisk pace, and most skill-building drills were completed in a short period of time. This was done to keep us focused on the skill and use time efficiently so that we could scrimmage and become automatic with the skills while playing basketball.

When I think about planning for fluency instruction, the structure of basketball practice influences my thinking. I work with my students in short bursts of learning, consolidating skills and strategies that lead to fluency and building students' reading and writing stamina. As teachers, we need to plan for short bursts of learning that enable students to build stamina and become fluent readers and writers.

Gayle and I plan for these short bursts of instruction by first thinking about the skill, then which instructional setting (whole class, small group, or individual) will allow our students to learn and practice this skill. Automaticity with word recognition, spelling, and writing on demand are areas of instruction we target during short, focused lessons. The skills learned during these sessions allow our students to read for extended periods of time during reading workshop and sustain their writing for long stretches during writing workshop.

When planning for fluency instruction, we look for opportunities to foster students' automaticity with print, increase their reading rate, and read in meaningful phrased units. Richard Allington (2001, p. 75) reminds us that "providing children access with appropriately leveled texts and a non-interruptive reading environment typically produces profound changes in reading fluency and self-monitoring."

Of course, there isn't any right time to teach fluency. Instead, you have to look at your daily schedule and consciously plan for fluency while seizing teachable moments to stress the importance of fluency instruction. Brief fluency lessons occur during content studies and reading or writing workshops. Prior to these lessons, Gayle and I have informally assessed our students, found a specific focus for fluency instruction, and then decided which grouping structure would help us effectively and efficiently support our students. We have found that working within the context of our thematic studies or workshops allows students to quickly practice skills and then use them for purposeful reading or writing. Gayle and I adopted this thinking after reading Stanovich's seminal article (1980), "Toward an Interactive-Compensatory Model of Individual Differences in the Development of Reading Fluency." We want to build fluency skills so that our students can keep pace with their peers, think about the same content, and use most of the workshop time for personal, purposeful reading and writing.

Gayle's students scatter about the classroom, using the entire space for personal reading during independent reading time. As the students leave the meeting area, Gayle reminds them to use punctuation to guide their voices, a fluency concept she has demonstrated while reading aloud *The Other Side.* Some students have been reading quickly, not fluently. They read through punctuation, sometimes getting confused because one idea runs into the next or the intended meaning was altered. This will be the focus for her individual conferences. The small-group work will continue its thread of reading punctuation but will also extend to a word-solving strategy. Gayle wants her students to use repetitive patterns and the local context of the sentence to predict unknown words. She wants them to cue on the first letter(s) as they anticipate the next word, developing automaticity with print.

Gayle will mask a handful of words in the big book, *Oh No!* (Cairns 1987) She will mask the word *spot,* a repetitive word in the text. She will reveal the *s* and *p*, covering the rest of the word with a sticky note. She will mask this word on pages 4 and 6, knowing that students will have had an opportunity to read and internalize the pattern of this text. She will mask *dress* on page 10 and *place* on page 16, allowing students to use the meaning and structure of the text and picture to predict these words. Ellie, John, Seth, Tommy, and Alya will work together with Gayle in this flexible group.

Gayle will begin this short lesson with the students writing five frequent words on wipe-off boards. She wants to build the students speed in knowing these words that appear on the word wall. Then she prompts the group to write the high frequency word *see* at the top of their wipe-off board, underline the *s*, and then write words that begin with *s*. The group generates high frequency words *so, saw,* and *she,* copying from the word wall. They also independently come up with *sat, sand, sad, set, sit, Seth,* and *Stephanie.* Gayle brings closure to this segment of her lesson by prompting the kids to write *seen* and *seed.* The students easily add the final consonants, laughing that they should have remembered these words. The students read the big book with masked words and after about seven minutes, find their own places in the classroom to read independently.

Gayle scans the room noting where individuals and small groups are reading. She spots Sam sitting at a table by himself reading *Henry and Mudge in Puddle Trouble.* She makes her way over to the table, pulls up a chair alongside him and without asking, he reads orally from the middle of page 19. The text challenges Sam because he wants to read the line of text as a phrase. Gayle says, "Sam I like how you're reading the line of words together, listen to how I read the idea." Gayle reads, "One blue petal fell from his mouth into Henry's hand," from the book. "You didn't stop at the end of the line, Mrs. Brand," Sam comments. Sam reads to the end of the chapter similar to Gayle's model. He reflects, "I didn't have to reread so much, it was easier to follow the text."

Reading workshop ends with students sharing about how they used punctuation to understand their reading. Ellie, Seth, John, Tommy, and Alya share that while reading *Oh No!* there are red letters and an exclamation point to tell them how to read the line. They think they should be reading them with voices that convey something is wrong, not just excitement. The students move next to word study. The group will work on making words with magnetic letters from the rime, *eat*.

I will also nurture fluency development by bringing Matt, T.J., Alyssa, and Alex together as a group. I will use shared reading to reading with them the *Time for Kids* article, "Saving Our National Parks." I will demonstrate fluent reading by pausing and thinking about big ideas. I will begin by reading the title and subtitles and reading captions while looking at pictures. I will think out loud about what I think this article will teach me.

My reading begins by stating my purpose for reading. My purpose for reading this article is to find out how we can save our national parks. The reason this is my purpose is because I noticed the subtitle, "What Can Be Done." I record this on the chart and begin reading. I read the article while the group follows along. Students stop me to reread sections or record important information on the chart. I bring closure to the lesson by asking the kids what they noticed. "I need to spend more time looking at what I'm going to read before reading it," Matt comments. Alyssa reflects, "You read to the end of the sentence before stopping, not the end of the line. I need to look for periods and question marks." T.J. reports, "I'm going to write a purpose now when I read. This will help me focus on why I'm reading. I won't stop so much."

The students join the rest of their classmates, sharing what they learned about national parks and reading fluently. As a class, we debrief our reading by writing a summary about national parks' renewable resources. We use shared writing to write this summary. While rereading the summary, we discuss punctuation and fluent reading. The discussion reinforces the day's fluency thinking.

Gayle's primary-grade classroom also has collections of texts used for curriculum content work organized in text sets. She may spend more time reading aloud texts from these baskets than I do. Gayle's text sets include big books that she uses for shared reading. She uses shared reading to introduce key ideas and develop schema and background knowledge that help her students learn vocabulary and ideas needed to read texts from the text set fluently. These primary-age students learn the importance of text features (pictures, captions, titles, and headings) as they read information for a variety of purposes.

Gayle not only uses big books during curriculum content study, but also uses an overhead projector to share texts. She demonstrates fluent reading, reading ideas by pointing or using an index card for reading a line at a time to focus her class on the text. By introducing key curriculum ideas and vocabulary in a shared format, she helps her students to read these ideas fluently. This helps her students internalize vocabulary and nonfiction written language forms.

Word Power—Building Words

Word study is an important component of students learning to become fluent. Automatic word recognition and spelling strategies allow readers and writers to focus on understanding texts or crafting their ideas on a page. Even though we both have a ten- to fifteen- minute Word Study Block as part of our day, we have found it beneficial to support groups of students with additional short, focused word-building lessons. We feel guilty pulling students away from their reading during the reading workshop for a word-building lesson. But, we keep in mind that these groups typically are together for about a week, for no more than five to ten minutes each day. What students learn enables them to develop automaticity with print so they can sustain their reading and build a reading stamina.

Gayle and I look at our students' reading and writing miscues (misspellings), pauses, and their body language, such as shoulder shrugs, as windows into their thinking. This information helps us form a hypothesis about why our students are not fluid readers or writers.

One area of concern for both of us is that some of our students do not understand the generative nature of how words work. When our students come to unfamiliar or unknown words, they do not always use their word knowledge to read the baffling word. These same students do not always use what they know about high frequency and single-syllable words to spell. Students may be aware of syllable breaks in words, yet not recognize the word part in this context. They may search for little words in big words and find them, but have trouble pronouncing or blending the parts together as they attempt to decode a challenging word. Since some of our students do not understand how knowing one word helps them read or write many words, we periodically conduct short word building lessons. These lessons last approximately five to ten minutes.

These lessons are grounded in student assessments; we work to untangle our students' confusion of the generative nature of how words work. Our goal

71

is to support students in developing understanding of the concept "If you know one word, you know many words." Depending on the experience of our learners and the sight vocabulary, we pick a high frequency word that students will be expected to know. It becomes an exemplar word that will anchor their thinking to read and write a myriad of words.

The first day or two of instruction begins by telling the students the key word, and then having the students write this on wipe-off boards. We use white boards because students enjoy this medium, write quickly, and can erase quickly—all unwritten goals of these lessons. Then we dictate words that are related to the key word. Changing the first or last letter, vowels, adding prefixes or suffixes, using a single syllable word to write multisyllabic words or compound words are all options in planning word-building lessons. Student engagement is high during these lessons—they comment to us, discuss with their peers what they are noticing/learning, and anticipate words they may be asked to write (sometimes adding to our lists). To bring closure to the lesson, we quickly whip around the group, sampling each student, asking them to comment on their learning. We like to repeat initiating activities so students can consolidate confusions from the first day. We can also react to student challenges and allow students to build a more solid foundation of knowledge prior to extending their thinking.

Key Words

Short Vowel Patterns

black	van	flap	tell	nest	quick
hill	pin	think	rip	sit	drop
not	duck	bug	jump	dunk	

Long Vowel Patterns

mail	rain	make	whale	name	date
say	treat	twice	slide	fight	mine
joke	more	use			

Figure 4.1 Key Words

By the third day of word building, the lesson format shifts from the teacher dictating words to the students independently creating their own lists of words, and challenging each other to see who can have the longest list using the assigned time.

"At the top of your board write the word *look*," Gayle directs her small group.

While the small group quickly writes *look*, Gayle notices Niko having trouble forming *k*, so she slides next to him and quickly forms a *k* on his board and asks him to try it again. He studies her model, moves his marker like Gayle did, making a well-formed *k*. It is a letter that Niko has difficulty forming, and he has challenged himself to improve writing it because it is in his name. "That was faster and neater that time, Niko, just like you have been practicing with your name." He smiles as the lesson moves forward.

"Now, use the next two minutes to write as many words as you can by using *look*," a familiar prompt that signals the group to begin.

Gayle watches, her clipboard ready to record observations, as her students create lists similar to the model she provided by dictating to them the last two days. About a minute into their list-making she notices her students moving beyond her model, writing words she did not think they knew. "I like how you added *s* to *hook* to make *shook*," she celebrates with Tommy. The lists range from nine to fifteen words, and there are a few surprises, like *spooky, crook,* and *lookout,* which show students' independent thinking. Gayle brings closure to the lesson by asking the students to review their classmates lists and state a word that was written that surprised them.

The fourth day is similar in structure and format to the third day with one exception, the use of prompting questions. Gayle uses prompts to extend her group's thinking, build longer lists, and help them internalize questions they can ask themselves about words.

"Erase your board and write *look* at the top. Underneath *look* write a word that has a blend to start the word."

John writes *brook* and includes *Brooke*. "There are two ways to write brook," is his spontaneous reaction.

Ellie has written *shook*, listens to John's comment, and adds these words to her list.

"Now I want to challenge you. Begin writing *look*, but change the ending to *se*. Niko tries to pronounce the word, uttering "lose." "Niko that is so close, try again and think about *look*," Gayle coaches him. Niko listens to her demonstration and echoes "loose," then mumbling, "look, loose" a few times, practicing what he has just learned.

The fifth day is an extension of the third and fourth days. Gayle has the students write *look* at the top of their white boards and then spend two minutes generating words and creating longer lists. They ask themselves the prompting questions Gayle has used in small-group work and also during other word work sessions and conferences. The small-group work ends with Gayle creating a list using all the words from the students' lists to create a summary chart. The debriefing session again asks students to reflect about what they have learned and how they can use this thinking, information which they will include on the chart. This chart is shared with the whole class at the end of reading workshop as a celebration of learning. Students that were not part of the group are in the habit of offering words for these charts. The chart becomes part of the word-rich walls, referred to during many other instructional contexts.

Word-Building Prompts

- Write a word like the key word.
- Write as many words as you can in the next minute that are like the key word.
- Change the first letter. What word did you write?
- Change the last letter. What word did you write?
- Change the vowel. What word did you write?
- Change the first letter to a blend. What word did you write?
- Add a prefix to the word. What word did you write?
- Add a suffix. What word did you write?
- Add another syllable to the key word. What word did you write?
- Use what you know about the key word to write a two-syllable word (three-syllable word). What word did you write?
- **Reflection prompts:** How are the words you wrote like the key word? What did you learn from building words? How will this help while you are reading? Writing?

Figure 4.2 Word-Building Prompts

In my fifth-grade classroom, I work through a similar multiple-day word-building schedule. I target a high frequency word that has many possibilities to build other words. Words that I typically target are frequency words that have

---

Example List Made From *Use* as the Key Word

uses	*used*	*using*	*user*	*useful*	*usual*	*usually*
unusual	*confuse*	*fuse*	*fused*	*obtuse*	*acute*	*accuse*
accusing	*accused*	*accuser*	*useless*			

Figure 4.3 Key Words

Five Days of Word Building

Day 1   *Students are prompted to write a key word at the top of a white board.*

Teacher dictates words for students to write that are related to key word.

Day 2   *Students are prompted to write the same key word at the top of a white board.*

Teacher dictates some words for students to write and prompts students to generate a related word.

Day 3   *Students write the same key word at the top of a white board without prompting.*

Teacher dictates two related words and then prompts students to write as many related words as possible in two minutes.

Day 4   *Students write the same key word at the top of a white board without prompting.*

Teacher prompts students to write as many related words as possible in two minutes. To extend the list, teacher prompts students to extend their thinking.

Day 5   *Students write the same key word at the top of a white board without prompting.*

Teacher prompts students to write as many related words as possible in two minutes. Create an anchor chart of words students generated. Hang the chart in the room as a reference and for future additions.

Figure 4.4 Five Days of Word Building

long vowel patterns that still confuse my students. We build from these single-syllable words by changing the beginning and ending, adding affixes, writing polysyllabic words, and including words that have a long vowel pattern in the second and third syllable.

The goal of this type of instruction is automaticity. We want our students to know how to look at word parts and use what they know about the word to decode or write words. I have learned that by writing these words, students are attending to aspects of print they may have ignored. These lessons are short and support independent reading and writing.

Small-Group Reading Along

Pulling groups to differentiate instruction is tricky work, especially with older students. These groups rarely happen before the second month of school. I know that with both primary- and intermediate-age learners, having a supportive learning community is essential to differentiated group work. When I pull a small group, I ask a handful of students by name if they would like to join me. It is rare for a student to refuse this invitation. I think this offer is a welcome relief for those working at frustration level. As the group is assembling, I extend the invitation to the rest of the class, and I am surprised by students who join the group.

We are leaving our morning circle time, and I have just assigned my students to read 2½ pages from their social studies text, which introduces them to pilgrimages as a reason for English immigration to the new world. Jenna, Jessica, and Ben approach me. "Can we read with you today?" they inquire. I look towards James; he grabs his social studies text and joins us. I ask, "Would anyone like to read with us?" T.J., Matt, Alyssa, and Brady enlarge our circle. I turn to the assigned page, read the title, *Pilgrims,* scan the picture, look up, seeing my students doing similar things and hear Ben ask Joseph, "Do you think we should set a purpose?" Joseph shrugs as Alyssa states, "Let's use the focus question as our purpose." Heads nod until Jessica squeaks, "No, I want to only learn about the Pilgrims, I'll wait until our group discussion to learn about immigration." I interject, "Maybe Jess is right, thinking about one idea will help our reading." My students are getting the hang of this, I reflect, as I begin reading to them. We are thinking about pilgrims, and I am introducing the idea of a pilgrimage.

The reading-along begins with setting a purpose for our reading, similar to class read-aloud, and something I prompt my students to think about when reading independently. I then read the text fluently, adjusting my speed. I stop, ask myself questions about the text or think aloud, and summarize what I have just read. While I am reading, the small group is reading along with me. I am explicit with students, helping them experience the feel and sound of fluent reading.

Calling their attention to my fluent reading is important to building their fluency. I ask the students to notice how I read phrases, used the punctuation to guide my voice, paused to think, and summarized what I just read. We also discuss how I used this information or what I just learned in the text to predict what could come next or to reread. These are all reading habits I want my students to use.

Monitoring students' attention during this time is a challenge, but worth my time if I can divide my attention a few ways. I try to notice their eyes. Are they reading along in phrases? Are they using print cues, attempting to decode unknown words prior to my reading, then allowing my reading to confirm their confusions? Are my students reading ahead, anticipating what will come next, learning language patterns of nonfiction texts? Yet I trust my students are taking the opportunity to learn from this experience. It is during these times that Malcolm Mitchell's words (Fried 2001, p. 152) reverberate in my mind, "Kids are imitators. And when they identify with you and with what makes you think and act, they want a piece of that."

Rereading is also a routine strategy that is demonstrated and practiced during read-aloud group instruction. Since the texts that I am reading are novel and introduce new ideas to the learners, rereading makes sense as part of this instruction. I try to slip in one or two opportunities for authentic rereading. In this setting, our rereading clarifies thinking, enabling the learners to connect their purpose for reading to their understanding. I encourage students to reread orally. When I do ask the students to read orally, I prefer choral reading so that group members can scaffold each other. The oral reading is one more time to notice and record students' phrasing and automaticity with print and monitor their fluency development and the effects of my instruction.

Timed Writing

We both ask our students to write often each day. They write for a variety of purposes and at different instructional times. They write to demonstrate what they understand in content studies and math. They choose what to write about during writing workshop. And at other times, our students write on demand from our prompts. We realize that our students need to write with both speed and clarity. Murray (2002, p. 146) reminds us of the importance of writing

77

quickly. "Most writers of articles and short stories try to finish a draft at a sitting. They write as fast as they can, allowing the momentum of their writing to carry them forward."

So, we ask our students to write to the bottom of the page or the end of a draft or an idea to help them develop fluency. This is not an easy task, especially for some primary-age students. To make this task manageable, Gayle may use an egg timer and set it for a short duration as a student or group of students builds stamina and stays focused on writing. This support facilitates their fluent writing development.

The egg timer strategy works well for Seth, especially when completing an assigned task fluently. One assignment Seth has difficulty with is "Look, Say, Cover, Write, and Check." This is a word-work task. Gayle asks Seth to move his chair directly in front of the pocket chart. Gayle reviews with Seth the eight new word-wall words that the class has been studying. They are not yet included with the other word-wall words; instead these words are written on index cards and placed in a pocket chart so the students can easily see them during the study.

Gayle prompts Seth to read the words by pointing to each one. Seth does this without a problem. Then she coaches him, "Seth, I am going to set this timer for eight minutes. I want you to neatly copy each new word three times. Make sure you check your spelling." Gayle sets the timer and watches as Seth begins copying the first word, *here*. Gayle watches him copy it once, moves around the room to monitor her other students doing other word-work activities. She returns to Seth after about a minute and a half. He is now copying the second word, *little*. "Come on Seth, you need to work a bit quicker, you only have six minutes left." Gayle returns after a minute and coaxes him to work faster. When the timer beeps Seth has almost finished. He gets an extra few seconds to finish. Tommy tells Seth, "You did better today, you almost made it. You're getting faster."

Seth isn't the only student in Gayle's class who needs a gentle reminder from a timer. This timer is a temporary device that helps students develop their own monitoring strategies. At the beginning of the year as Gayle's students are learning how to complete their reading log, she uses an egg timer so they know what five minutes feels like. After a week or two, only a small group of students needs this device to keep them focused on finishing their task.

Once a week, Gayle has her students work in their writing notebooks to "pump up" their writing. Tommy, Seth, Kara, and Ellie may not complete one sentence during a ten-minute writing spree while the rest of the class write between six and eight sentences. Gayle has the four of them sit at a table that

78

has the egg timer. The egg timer helps them pace their writing, getting their pumped-up ideas written down on paper fluently. They write two or three sentences as they challenge each other to see not only how much they wrote, but how detailed their writing is.

In my fifth-grade classroom, my students often write on demand, demonstrating what they understand from content reading or to summarize what they learned while researching a topic. I give the students five minutes for what I call a "rapid write." At first the students do not get very far with their writing, but after a week not only do they complete their writing, but they actually ask if they will be doing a "rapid write." Writing quickly, letting their ideas flow as they build momentum, has helped students develop as fluent writers.

Reading to Get to the Bottom of It

We also challenge students to "read on demand"—students read short meaningful texts within a time limit. The texts students read on demand are short and easy to read, yet present ideas and concepts we want students to think through. Short bursts of reading on demand help students understand the importance of reading ideas and learning how paragraphs, sentences, and phrases are writers' tools. These tools are used by writers to craft ideas, ideas we read together by reading in phrase units to understand the text. While reading these passages we adjust our pace, speeding up or slowing down, to help make sense of the ideas and our purpose for reading.

"Reading to get to the bottom of it" is just that, a timed reading in which students read to the bottom of the page. "The bottom of it," though, has a dual meaning, referring also to unearthing the big ideas in the reading passage. As with all reading in our classrooms, we set purposes for reading and adjust them while we read, and focus our thinking. In this setting we impose a purpose for the reading, since we are requesting the reading. As with most activities, students begin to take ownership and soon we are negotiating the purpose. Empowerment is liberating to students, slowing down even our well-intentioned demands.

"This morning we are going to read to the bottom of it. We are going to read our *Time for Kids*, 'After the Waves.' We are going to read and think about how people are helping out after the tsunami." The magazine is passed around the circle. With one eye, Gayle monitors the flow of magazines and with the other reads the front cover, "After the Waves. Giant waves hurt many people. The world is working to help. This girl in India chooses from clothes that people gave."

"Wow, she looks poor," she remarks. "She has a lot of clothes to choose from," Kara reports. "Hey, Mrs. Brand, you didn't read the top," John cleverly comments. "You're right, John, thank you." Gayle reads the forgotten line, "People get food they need."

After taking a moment for the full text to be thought through, Gayle continues, "We are going to read to the bottom of page three and think about how people are helping people that had problems because of the tsunami. I am going to give you only five minutes to read it the first time through. We will use this article to think about how we can reach out."

The first- and second-grade students spend the next five minutes reading the two assigned pages. Students use silent reading, whisper reading, choral reading, and independent oral reading to learn about how the world helps tsunami victims.

Gayle slides next to Ellie, clipboard in hand, listening to her oral reading. She notes that Ellie is reading line by line, not always in phrased units, but wonders if the format of the text has forced Ellie to read in this manner. She also records miscues, noticing a pattern: geographic names were a challenge, yet Ellie did use word parts to attempt to read them. *Ten* for Tennessee, *in* and *do* for Indonesia, along with *May* for Malaysia were signals that word building was helping Ellie become an independent reader. Even though Ellie read only half the assignment, this was an improvement. Ellie realized it and commented on it to Gayle when she informed the class that five minutes had passed.

Debriefing the assigned reading, Gayle begins by announcing that she heard lots of good reading. She adds, "I think it was interesting to see that people who finished early found each other and discussed the map." As Gayle finishes, Tommy clarifies, "We were trying to figure out how the little map fits in with the big map. We were thinking how lucky we are to live on the other side of the world." "We are fortunate that Ohio only had a little snow," Gayle responds.

"What were the challenges with the reading?" she inquires. Students chorally reflect, "The names of those places." Gayle admits she still has trouble with some of the names, compliments Ellie for using word parts and not letting the names stop her reading. The kids cluster by a chart and list important ways people are helping tsunami victims. They do this by rereading excerpts from the article. They reread their list, suggest that this article should remain at school in reading baskets because they need to read it again and discuss this more. Students place the magazines in book baskets as they transition to math. While Gayle reflects about what she noticed and heard from her students, she begins thinking about how to incorporate shared reading with word building.

In my fifth-grade room we use a very similar format for "Reading to Get to the Bottom of It." Previewing the front cover and weaving in unfamiliar vocabulary while negotiating the purpose for reading are rituals that help my students become independent fluent readers. I also take the time to monitor oral reading behaviors. Since my students are all reading silently, I have taught them to whisper read when I sit next to them at their desk. I record reading behaviors to use during our debriefing or during a reading conference. I have adopted this neutral stance because the students are trying to put together a fluent reading process and I do not want to interfere with other students who are sitting nearby.

This story telling not only helps develop oral reading fluency, but develops writing fluency. Students learn how to transform an idea to spoken language and then written language. Gayle demonstrates this process, rotating around the group, writing different students' stories on a chart. These stories vary in length, typically four to six sentences, similar to her expectation in writing workshop. The stories are read chorally as students begin to monitor their fluency using the scale they developed. Students reread these charts during buddy reading and during writing workshop, borrowing ideas and sentences as they revise their ideas in their own writing. Oral language work also occurs during the writing workshop mini-lesson when Gayle asks the students to share out loud what they are going to write about before going to write.

Also, during writing workshop each child has an assigned sharing day. Students read out loud pieces of writing that are finished, works in progress, or part of a piece of writing. On their assigned sharing day, they are reminded to use the last three to five minutes of writing workshop to reread and practice what they will be sharing out loud. While students are reading their writing orally, classmates listen intently, monitoring first if they understand the story and how fluently the students read their own writing. Students use the oral language rubric as a way to provide feedback to one another.

Another oral language opportunity Gayle uses is called building an idea. It helps her students become fluent writers and move from thought to spoken words and involves using the word wall. Gayle supports her students' use of the word wall as a tool for thinking by selecting a word for students to orally use in a sentence. "Can anyone use the word-wall word *were* in a sentence?" A student responds, "We *were* happy." After hearing the simple sentence she challenges them to "pump up" that sentence—i.e., "We *were* happy at school today because we got an extra recess." This strategy is used often in the first half of the year. While students are listening to each other share during writing workshop, one comment may be to "pump up" a part of the writing. Students

81

internalize this prompt and become more fluent in their writing because they are mentally "pumping up" their sentences before they even write them down. Students also reread their own writing, asking themselves if they should add more and revise their writing.

Whether it is a primary or intermediate grade classroom, we feel short bursts of reading and writing on demand mirror real-world reading and writing. They also prepare our students for the demands of standardized testing. The reading and writing that students do on demand is a small percentage of the reading they do throughout the day. We use this time to build a skill set so that students can read and write fluently during content inquiries, as well as in reading and writing workshop.

The lessons that follow focus on using short bursts to build reading and writing stamina.

Lesson 4.1
Reading to the Bottom of It

Thoughts: Reading nonfiction and content texts fluently is a challenge for many of our students. We challenge our students to read on demand in short bursts as they develop fluency while reading nonfiction texts. Our goal is to get them to read ideas, paragraphs, sentences, and phrases by reading in short bursts. "Reading to the bottom of it" is a timed reading where students work on their reading pace and uncover big ideas as well.

Planning

Be prepared to demonstrate fluent reading of ideas using an enlarged text.

Prepare an overhead copy of a single-page *Time For Kids* article, *Write TFK* or *Nonfiction TFK* text.

Big books work well in primary grades.

What it looks and sounds like

We begin "reading to the bottom of it" activities by previewing text features (title, sub-titles, captions, pictures, maps, graphs, etc.) prior to reading. This helps activate schema as we set a purpose for reading. We begin by prompting students, "Today you are going to read to the bottom of this text. While you are reading, I want you to think about _____. You have five minutes to read to the bottom." Students read the text silently for five minutes. Students who finish early reread the passage, preparing for our discussion of the big ideas.

While students are reading, we take the opportunity to monitor students' oral reading. We target one or two students, listening to the child orally read a few sentences or a paragraph. We record fluent reading behaviors and miscues.

After five minutes we conclude the silent reading and ask the students, "What were the challenges with your reading?" Students often comment on words that were challenging to decode or words they did not understand. We use a wipe-off board to help students with decoding challenges. We reread the challenging parts of the text, getting students to think first about meaning and how they can use text clues. During the rereading, students notice punctuation that affected their reading.

We bring closure by asking students, "What did you learn about yourself as a reader?" After a quick sharing, we nudge thinking towards goal setting, "What could you do differently the next time you read?" Again students share and we record anecdotes to be used for planning purposes and individual conferences.

Lesson 4.2
Pump It Up: Writing

Thoughts: We have found that our students often write simple sentences that do not describe the ideas they want to convey. We ask our students to reread their writing and think about places that could "pump up their writing" and make it more interesting or rich. We demonstrate how to take a simple piece and add some "meat" to it. We then ask students to take a draft and find places to "pump up" their own writing. Students learn to fluently apply this strategy while writing first drafts or as they revise their first drafts.

Planning

Select a piece of writing that has many simple sentences. Copy this text on a chart or overhead.

Students select or create their own writing.

What it looks and sounds like

We bring the students together and use shared reading to read a piece of first draft writing that lacks detail or description. We then prompt students to reread the passage, thinking about a place where the writing could be revised or "pumped up". Once the group has agreed on a place to revise the writing, we orally list possibilities and then discuss how that will make the writing more detailed and help the reader understand the idea.

Then students bring a current draft and apply the same thinking. Once students "pump up" their writing, we share first drafts and revisions, thinking about how the revisions helped the reader understand the writing.

We bring closure to the lesson by asking the students, "How will you use 'pump up your writing' while composing and revising?" Students talk about how this strategy can get them to focus their writing on ideas and think about important details and descriptions.

An Alternative: Once students are comfortable with "pump it up" as a writing strategy, we may bring a group together and have them craft an observation or reflection in a Writer's Notebook or on a wipe-off board. Once they have their first draft down, we either prompt them to "pump up their writing" or share and then "pump it up." We discuss first drafts and revisions, guiding students to think about how they are helping readers understand ideas. The rereading and discussion help our students develop not only fluent writing strategies, but fluent oral reading.

Lesson 4.3
Page Layout

Thoughts: Many times our students dive into the text without viewing text features and struggle to understand what they are reading. To help our students set a purpose for their reading and build schema for a text, we ask students to use text features. These text features help our students anticipate ideas and predict what will come next, as they read fluently.

Planning

Be prepared to demonstrate how you use text features to develop schema and purpose for your own reading.

Prepare an overhead copy of a *TFK* article and student copies of the same *TFK*. You might also use an informational big book that has a variety of text features or a *TFK* Big Picture.

What it looks and sounds like

Students need to have an authentic purpose for reading a text. One of those purposes is to understand the big idea. Previewing a text by examining the page layout and developing schema for the text helps students set a purpose for why they will read a text. Students' schema and purpose helps them anticipate ideas as they read and develop fluent reading habits.

Guiding students to think about the title, captions, subtitles, side bars, maps, graphs, and labels helps develop fluency. We begin by getting students to carefully consider the title and its meaning. As we are preparing to read the title, we ask, "What do you think the title means?"

While discussing the title, we prompt students to think about other text features that support the text. "Read the subtitles and captions and think how these go with the title" helps students connect text features with the title.

Then we ask students, "What do you think you will learn from reading this article?" After discussion, we follow up with, "What is your purpose for reading?" Students then read the text independently. We discuss the text and reread parts that were interesting or confusing. We end the reading by asking the reflective question, "How did looking at the text features help you read this text fluently?"

By building schema and getting students to think about vocabulary and ideas, students will read more fluently as they work to understand the text.

Lesson 4.4
Word Work: Generating Words

Thoughts: Fluent readers are able to read unknown words by looking for known patterns or chunks. Some students may need explicit guidance in how to look for patterns in words. We use rime patterns of single-syllable words as a starting point to help students see patterns in words and connect their understanding to unknown words. We use running records of students' oral reading and their writing samples as assessment tools to identify students who need this type of focused instruction and what rime patterns to focus on.

Planning

Assess your students' oral reading and writing to form groups.

Collect wipe-off boards.

What it looks and sounds like

We pick one rime pattern that we will use for approximately a week. The first few lessons require the teacher to dictate words that are related to the targeted rime pattern. As students understand the task and possibilities for connecting to the rime pattern, they take over this task. We use white boards so that students can write quickly, monitor their own work, and make corrections.

This short burst lesson begins by dictating the key word. "Write _____ at the top of your board. Write it again more neatly. Write it one more time, more quickly and neatly." This focuses the students' attention on letter formation and the entire word. Then we dictate approximately five other words that have the same rime pattern. In primary grades, we may only change the beginning consonant. We eventually move to changing the beginning and ending consonants. In intermediate grades, we not only change the beginning and ending, but use multi-syllable words and affixes. We summarize the first day's session by asking, "What did you notice about all the words?" Students discuss the rime pattern, often relating it to the sound of vowels. We bring closure to the lesson by prompting, "Do you know any other words that could fit this pattern?"

The following days we pass on more responsibility by asking students to generate words that they can connect to this rime pattern. We then prompt students to write other words as we assess how they are using what they are learning about generating words.

At the end of the week we ask the students to write the key word and write as many words as possible in a short burst. We then chart the words.

ONGOING ASSESSMENT FOR TARGETED INSTRUCTION

5

"In order to ensure that fluency instruction is included in the curriculum, it is necessary to create strategies that are classroom-friendly and that can be easily integrated within current literacy practice."

Melanie Kuhn, *The Reading Teacher,* 2004/2005

Fluency is not one skill, but the orchestration of many skills. These include word identification strategies, sight vocabulary, prosody, expressive and phrased reading that sounds like spoken language, and ways to demonstrate the reader is making sense of the reading material. These skills and strategies are teachable. Providing multiple opportunities for kids to read and write for a variety of purposes throughout the school day will support students' development of fluent reading and writing. We also believe that we need to provide instruction during the day for specific teaching of fluency.

Large-group instruction including read-aloud, shared reading, and shared writing will not meet the needs of all our learners. We have to differentiate instruction, supporting learning in flexible groups and individual conferences. Gayle and I plan for small-group fluency instruction by using a variety of assessments that capture the students' strategies while reading or writing. When listening to students read, we listen for phrased reading and note automaticity with print. Running records, student reading logs, and our anecdotal notes make it possible to consider students' reading rates and fluency and how it affects comprehension. By listening to students read a variety of texts and genres, we monitor their understanding and fluency. This helps us accumulate snapshots of their reading processes.

We have also observed our students' writing, noticing their writing habits, analyzing their encoding strategies, and looking for patterns in their spelling errors. We watch students write, observing how they record their thinking on a page. Some write slowly, laboring over each letter and word. Others write their thoughts quickly in phrases, sentences, and pages of thought. We spend the first few weeks of school getting to know our students' literacy knowledge and developing a literacy profile.

Gayle uses a grid with each student's name on it to record reading behaviors and also uses running records as formative assessment tools. This helps her develop insights about each child as a reader and note fluid reading. While listening for fluency, she notices automatic word recognition skills and strategies and whether the reading sounds like spoken language. Using language from a fluency rubric (see Appendix), Gayle notes whether the student reads in meaningful phrases and is guided by punctuation. She groups words together on running records and in her anecdotal notes so she has a record of how students are grouping words while reading. Miscues and self- corrections provide her with a window into the child's word-solving skills and strategies.

Literacy Profile

Anecdotal Notes

- Snippets of talk
- Notes of student's fluency while reading (fiction, nonfiction, *TFK*, poetry)
- Reading observations
- Writing observations

Running Records

- Students' reading log
- Writing samples
- District assessments

Figure 5.1 Literacy Profile

When I sit next to one of my fifth-grade students, I try to listen to him read orally, somewhere between 100 and 200 words of continuous text. This should take a minute or two if the student is reading fluently and at an appropriate pace. My observations are recorded in my planning notebook and used in planning and conferring with a student. I also record miscues and group how the student reads words so that I have a record of his fluent reading. Over the course of a few weeks, I attempt to hear my students read narrative texts, nonfiction, and poetry.

When assessing a student's oral reading, I listen to her read an introductory paragraph, recording her fluency as she orients herself to a text. If the text is at an appropriate level, I'll prompt the student to read silently, noting her reading pace while silently reading along with her. After a page or two of silent reading, we discuss the reading so I can monitor understanding. I finish this type of informal assessment by listening to the child read another section of the text orally, another 100 to 200 words. I like to compare the fluency of both oral readings. Students who have difficulty with fluency either read quickly or slowly. This type of assessment takes approximately five to seven minutes and can be done as students read curriculum and self-selected reading materials.

My students read on demand most mornings from short texts or poems. This is one period of time I can count on to assess fluent reading, reading rate, and understanding. I provide many opportunities for my students to read short texts at the beginning of the year. A big challenge is not selecting texts that are too difficult which can force students to read at frustration level and possibly shut down.

We both have a reading workshop that includes a long block of time for self-selected independent reading. We want our students to learn how to monitor their independent reading rate and the books they choose to read. If we are developing independent fluent readers, then students can be responsible for this aspect of their reading. Our goal is to help students understand the relationship between fluency and pacing as they build reading stamina and learn how to choose appropriate texts. We have developed short reading log sheets (see Appendix) that students use daily to monitor how many pages they have read and to record their thinking. Over the years, students' input and feedback have helped us arrive at our current form. This form is short so that students can spend most of their time reading, pausing periodically to jot down thoughts and demonstrate their understanding.

The reading log is a tool that helps students learn about themselves as readers. Students use these reading logs to monitor their own progress and set goals and as a tool to talk about their reading with a book buddy. Students reflect on their reading rate/pace, fluency, and choice and understanding of texts in independent reading, as well as making goals. Prior to reading independently, my students state a daily reading rate/pace goal. Gayle's first-grade students challenge themselves, too, setting goals related to reading picture books or rereading books from baskets.

Peter Johnston's thinking about literacy assessment has influenced our reading log design. According to Johnston (2005, p. 685), "Classroom assessment can socialize children into monitoring and guiding their own literacy learning." While developing reading logs, we use student feedback to fine-tune them, trying to ensure that students can demonstrate understanding and that we notice their fluent reading and record and reflect on their reading pace.

Another important point he brought to our attention (p. 685) is, "Children struggling with literacy constantly turn to the teacher for feedback. This reliance on external monitoring indicates that children have assessed themselves as incapable of assessing their own learning. Turning this situation around requires teachers to view children as if they can know what they know, how they are doing, and how they can tell." Now when we plan for fluency focus lessons, we use our observations and records and students' own assessments of their reading to inform our decisions.

Students also use their reading log to consider the difficulty of a text. When Joseph, a fifth-grader, notices that he has only read three or four pages each day from a Sherlock Holmes book, I can confer with him about text difficulty. I begin this type of reading conference by having a student read orally.

Once again, listening to a child read between 100–200 words or a paragraph is enough. The oral reading with my note-taking allows me to help students monitor their reading. Once the reading is finished, I'll begin the conference by inquiring, "What did you notice about your reading?" My goal is to help students monitor their reading, noticing the text may be difficult because of the vocabulary, ideas, or density.

These are difficult conferences to have with students because you may tell them that they need to read an easier text. Students who struggle often do not want to lose face with their peers. There are situations when I may not ask the child to totally abandon the text, but suggest that this may be a book to read at home with a parent or older sibling. Another alternative that I have used only sparingly is to read the text with the student. I may do the bulk of the reading at the beginning of the book. Once the student becomes familiar with the characters and plot I fade away, allowing the student to develop independence. Gayle does similar co-reading with students. We may vary the co-reading where we read a sentence and then the student reads the next sentence, paragraph, or page, depending on the child's individual needs.

To help students understand the concept of reading rate and pace related to appropriate texts, I model this prior to reading aloud. "This afternoon while reading *Pictures of Hollis Woods,* I would like to read twenty pages. This includes the picture and the chapter," I announce to my students, turning the book sideways showing them what twenty pages looks like from this book. "I should be able to read this much aloud. The picture is short. While reading the picture sections, I have to really slow down," I add. Maggie blurts out, "I think that is too much. You will never read that." Savannah adds, "I agree with Maggie. We're going to find out what happened to Steven and Hollis, you can't read that fast." James reminds the group, "If we let Mr. Brand read and think out loud today then he can reach his goal. Yesterday we agreed we would only talk at critical times."

"You three all made good points. Today, I want to read and think out loud without too much talk. I want you to notice my reading pace, especially when I slow down and speed up." I read the text aloud, thinking out loud instead of the customary interactive discussion. James is perceptive, knowing that we have been talking a lot, making the reading too choppy and hard to understand.

When I am finished, I try to trigger discussion about pacing as it relates to understanding. The class notices there were times I read fluidly, not stopping to think for two or three pages. They also notice that sometimes I picked up the pace when my thinking was not clear, reading further to try to clarify. If this did not work, I went back and reread the section where I was confused, trying to clarify the meaning. This is a strategy that I will continually use with my students, demonstrating it during read-aloud and reemphasizing it during conferences. I pass out student reading logs, asking students their goals. Jessica and Jenna announce they are going to read faster, not stopping as much. Alex tells me she is going to move away from her friends so she isn't tempted to share her thinking with her friends until the end of reading time.

Small-Group Talk—A First Step Towards Fluency

Scanning through our assessments and student work, we look for students who have similar instructional needs. By sorting out patterns of students' confusion, our fluency lessons help students develop automaticity with print (including a sight vocabulary) and prosody, reading in meaningful phrases to make oral reading sound like oral language. The goal of these lessons is for students to orchestrate their word-solving skills with their oral language skills. We want them to read for meaning and think beyond the printed word.

We target these areas because they are hindering the students' fluent reading. These flexible groups are temporary adjustments to students' instruction and independent reading.

We also have students who are not fluent with their oral language, which affects their reading and writing fluency. Our instruction with these students helps them develop an ear for fluent language, in conversation and reading. Our first step is to begin with small-group conversation, having the students talk about themselves and tell life stories. While kids are "spinning their yarns," we note the cadence of their talk, noticing if and when their voice varies. Does the child talk with expression? The key to these conversations is two-fold, first having the group listen to the speaker and notice oral fluency before developing a rubric to describe rate and improve oral fluency. The second is to get the speaker to monitor his or her own speech patterns.

Demonstration is critical when helping students notice and name a behavior. I know that even with my fifth-graders, it is important that I demonstrate different speaking patterns. I name the behavior prior to demonstrating. Then I have students tell me characteristics they noticed that help them remember the named behavior. The descriptors are often the terms students use as we develop our rubric. I have found that using a descriptive

---

Oral Storytelling Rubric

4   *The speaker spoke in smooth phrases using expression. Ideas flowed, one after the other. It was easy to understand what the speaker was talking about.*

3   *The speaker talked fast, sometimes putting all their words together, making it hard to follow parts of the story. Most of the ideas flowed together. We only asked a couple questions to help us understand.*

2   *The speaker was choppy, putting a few words together at a time. Some of the ideas flowed together, but the speaker paused, trying to connect ideas. The speaker stuttered, using "um, um" or "like" to connect ideas. We had to ask the speaker a lot of questions to help us understand.*

1   *The speaker sounded like a robot, talking word by word. Ideas were mixed up. It was hard to follow the story.*

Figure 5.2 Oral Storytelling Rubric

sentence instead of numbers helps students internalize the behaviors they are working towards and does not put a value on what is "right."

This rubric is intentionally similar to a reading fluency scale. Our goal is to shift students' oral language pattern to aid them while reading. This may seem like something more appropriate for primary grades, but in my fifth grade I may have five or six kids that can benefit from small group talk as a tool for writing. The rubric helps my students understand what fluency sounds like, along with providing descriptors that guide their fluent reading and self-assessment.

Small-Group Instruction Focused on Prosody

Once students are familiar and comfortable with using an oral fluency scale as a tool to reflect on fluency while telling a story, we move on to focused fluent reading. The texts we use to focus on fluency instruction are easy. An easy text is one that a student can read with greater than 95 percent accuracy. Easy texts are used because our goal is fluent reading. We want students to read in meaningful phrases, paying attention to punctuation and using the meaning and structure to guide their interpretation of the text. For fifth-grade teachers, one resource for easy texts is the *Time For Kids (TFK)* from the grade level below you. The *TFK* has the same stories, usually shorter and with an easier vocabulary. My students have plenty of background with this text because of their exposure and discussion with the grade-level text. Other resources I try to use with my fifth-graders are picture books, poems, and, periodically, leveled texts.

Gayle uses similar texts; she also has little books, patterned books published by The Wright Group and Dominie Press and "PM Readers" published by Rigby. Big books that students read chorally, using each other as a resource, are another option. These books support fluent reading of ideas, sentences, and lines of print, as students use punctuation to guide their fluent reading. Students are exposed to frequently-written sentences and phrases, helping them internalize book language. Students also learn sight words that they repeatedly read and develop automaticity with print. Familiar texts work best. But, we know it is important that students learn how to be fluent on unseen, unfamiliar texts. Having students read a familiar text and then an unseen or unheard text is a format we both have used.

Demonstration is how we begin focused fluent oral reading instruction. During a demonstration, copies of the text are distributed to the small group of students so they can read along. They listen, notice how to read fluently,

93

and internalize the feel of fluent reading. Gayle brings together a group of first-graders who are reading word by word and laboring over the words, not the ideas. Gayle has decided to use the text, *Where are you going, Aja Rose?* by Joy Cowley. She has picked this familiar book because the text is written in a question-and-answer format. This book also supports choral reading because a group of students are asking the questions and each child can rotate through the role of Aja Rose, responding fluently.

"We are going to reread *Where Are You Going, Aja Rose?*" Gayle announces to the group. "When we read today, we are going to make our voices sound like we are talking. I will read the story through first and I want you to pay attention to how I read the story. When I am finished reading, I want you to use the storytelling rubric to describe my reading."

Before Gayle begins the demonstration, Ellie says, "Mrs. Brand, I noticed that when you read the title you paused at the mark before Aja Rose's name." "Ellie, I used the comma to help me sound like I was talking." Seth comments on the question mark, "Mrs. Brand made it sound like a question." Gayle reads the text, changing the tone of her voice to model reading the question and then as Aja Rose answering. Gayle's demonstration ends by inducing her group to think about her reading using the oral fluency rubric. Alya notices that Gayle's voice is fast, but easy to understand. Tommy asks if he can read the book with Gayle. She can read the questions, and he will respond as Aja Rose. Tommy reads with Gayle working hard to match his voice to the model Gayle demonstrated.

Gayle then pulls out multiple copies of the book *Bread*. This book will be an easy book for the kids to read fluently even though they have not seen or heard it before. The students whisper-read the book to themselves while Gayle moves to John and Alya, listening and recording their oral reading. Once the kids have finished their first reading, they move next to a buddy and whisper-read a favorite part of the text, explaining why they liked it while discussing the story. The fluency lesson concludes with each child reading a favorite part orally. The group listens to the reading and uses the oral fluency scale to monitor each student's fluent reading. These texts will be a model that Gayle uses to reinforce fluency lessons, anchoring her students' fluency understanding.

These lessons are short, follow a familiar pattern, and help students develop their reading voice. When planning for these lessons, we try to use a seven to ten minute time frame, plotting how to pull a group during independent reading and still leave plenty of time for students to read self-selected books independently.

Favorite Fluency Prompts

"Listen to me read it."

"Read along with me."

"Read it like you are telling a story."

"Make it sound like talking."

"Read it again and make it sound like talking."

"Can you show me with your fingers where the idea is written?"

"When you read, try putting ideas together."

"Pay attention to the punctuation while you are reading."

Figure 5.3 Favorite Fluency Prompts

We have found working with a group for a week or two will bring about a shift in their fluent reading, and then we use reading conferences to reinforce fluent reading.

We both use a variety of texts that students read when emphasizing prosody. When planning for oral reading lessons we have tried to remember Rob Tierney's (1990, p. 423) thinking, "Oral reading is a communication skill. It is a way of delivering information or providing entertainment to listeners. If used in this way, oral reading would seem best done for a specific purpose, and a student's performance would seem best evaluated in terms of its communicative value." Rereading could be done using:

- Reader's theater scripts
- Plays
- Puppet shows
- Books to be read to buddies
- Poems
- Student's published writing

This list is not exhaustive. We also like to have students use a pocket chart and reassemble poems, songs, or shared writing stories that we have cut up line by line. This strategy forces students to visually scan and quickly read a line of print, reassemble the message, and reread to monitor or self-correct for meaning. The goal is for students to reread lines of print so that their voices sound like speech.

Small-Group Instruction Focused on Automaticity with Print

Students who have large sight vocabularies and efficient decoding strategies read fluently. Building students' sight vocabulary and decoding strategies supports students' fluency development. When we pull students aside to form a group for extra word work, we need to be careful. First, we do not want to send the

Known High-Frequency Words

List 1

Name _____

Word	Can Read	Can Write
a		
at		
am		
an		
and		
can		
come		
do		
go		
he		
I		
in		
is		
it		
like		
look		
me		
my		
no		
see		
she		
so		
the		
to		
up		
we		

List 2

Name _____

Word	Can Read	Can Write
all		
are		
as		
be		
but		
came		
for		
from		
get		
got		
had		
has		
have		
her		
him		
his		
if		
of		
on		
there		
they		
this		
was		
with		
you		
your		

Figure 5.4 Known High Frequency Words

message that reading is getting the words right, even though fluent readers read with few errors. So, pulling words out of context is a short, temporary teaching strategy. We bring closure to word-work groups and emphasize fluent reading by rereading charts, big books, familiar texts, or short texts.

Like the prosody lessons, word-work lessons follow a typical flow— working with frequency words followed by word connections and then putting it all together by reading. The first step is choosing frequency words. We use oral reading notes, running records, and frequency word assessments to make this decision. We use frequency word assessments with students who are not fluent. In primary grades we have a high frequency word assessment (p. 96 and Appendix) we administer by using flash cards and noting known words. We use flash cards because we want to know frequent words known quickly. Working with intermediate-grade students I use words from the 500 most frequent words and administer it using flash cards. Many students can read these words, but not automatically.

These frequent words are often words that Gayle already has on her class word wall. She can then use this as a resource to help students learn these words. "Read the words on the wall while I point to them," she prompts her group. The group chorally reads the words, *come, here, said, this* and *your.* "Read them again faster," she coaches them. The students read this group of words three more times. Gayle mixes up the order she points to the words. "What did you notice about your reading?" she prompts. Kara announces, "We read faster each time." "Your pointing got faster and we got faster," John reports. "These words are automatic," Gayle informs the group. The lesson moves on with Gayle pointing to a variety of words on the wall. Gayle returns to words that are not automatic and makes a mental note to jot them down. Gayle then pulls out the big book, *Mud Walk* by Joy Cowley. The group reads this familiar book together. On page four she has covered up the letters *u* and *d*, exposing only the *m* for her students as a cue to read *mud*. On page five she has exposed the *g* of *good* and on page eight the *d* from *deeper.* This masking helps the students use the first letter as a cue when coming to an unfamiliar word. These words were chosen because they are at the end of the line. This allows the students to use the meaning and structure of the line to help their decoding, rather than word-by-word reading. The lesson ends with each student locating a frequency word in *Mud Walk* and then fluently reading the sentence the word is in.

Gayle targets five words for the group to work with. The words she targets for instruction are either high frequency words or exemplar words that she has noticed students spelling incorrectly or not reading automatically. A tool that makes this type of assessment manageable is a grid. Creating a grid with the

97

troublesome frequent word listed and students' names recorded underneath helps us plan and organize for instruction. We use writing along with reading as an assessment tool when evaluating students' knowledge of frequency words and word-building strategies.

We both value the power of writing and how it helps develop automaticity with print. Pinnell and Fountas (1998) remind us, "Word learning, letter learning, and learning about how print works are related bodies of knowledge. By using writing to help students develop automaticity with these two aspects of word knowledge we are guiding our students towards being fluent readers and writers. As the child learns to write he learns to take on the role of the reader." We believe in the reciprocal relationship between reading and writing, using writing to support fluent reading.

Small-Group Writing to Support Fluency

One of the biggest challenges we grapple with is when to pull a group of students for differentiated instruction. We realize the power of working with a small group of students, focusing their attention on a common misunderstanding and guiding them towards independence. During independent reading time we pull small groups of students for focused fluency lessons. Even though the students are writing words during a focused fluency lesson, they are developing strategies that will maintain them as readers. Students who are not developing a sight vocabulary of frequency words during word study lessons or while reading and writing need extra support to learn words.

We use a wipe-off board to support frequent word learning. We use wipe-off boards because students like this medium, the marker allows students to write quickly and smoothly, and they can quickly correct mistakes. Working with primary-age students, we use the class word wall as a tool to help support frequent word learning. Students sit so they are close to the word wall, but can see it in its entirety. The word wall will be a tool students use to monitor their accuracy, note where they misspelled a word and then correct the misspelled word.

Instruction begins by pointing and chorally reading words we will ask students to write on their boards. Then we prompt the students to write one of the words from the word wall. Students write the dictated word on the wipe-off board without copying from the word wall. Since our goal is to help children develop automaticity with frequent words, we do not want them to labor over copying it. This is a challenge at first for students, but once they learn the routine of this small-group work they challenge themselves and note spelling while reading. Students use the word wall to check the spelling of the dictated word. If a child has difficulty locating the word on the word wall, Gayle will point to the word on the wall, demonstrate copying it, and think out loud as she writes. Students fix their misspellings by writing the correct spelling underneath the misspelled word, comparing their spelling to the correct spelling. Students are then prompted to write the same word again. The kids often use their hand to cover up the original spelling as they rewrite the frequency word automatically. We often ask the students to write each word quickly approximately three times. Students understand from numerous demonstrations, prompts, and reminders that this does not mean sloppy or

---

A Five-Day Fluency Focus Plan—Primary

Day 1   *Students write five words from the word wall on wipe-off boards. These words have previously been introduced. Students talk about a picture and then use interactive writing to write about the picture.*

Day 2   *Students write the five words from day 1 on wipe-off boards. Students reread interactive writing from day 1, consider revising, and add another sentence.*

Day 3   *Students write each word from day 1, three times each. Students challenge themselves not to look at the word wall as a model, but to use as needed. Students reread interactive writing fluently. Students add another sentence or are introduced to another picture, talk about the picture, and then use interactive writing to write about it.*

Day 4   *Students write each word from day 1 three times each without using the word wall as a model, but use it to monitor their accuracy and make corrections if necessary. Students reread previous day's interactive writing, practicing fluent reading. Students add another sentence or are introduced to another picture, talk about the picture, and then use interactive writing to write about it.*

Day 5   *Students write each word from day 1 three times each without using the word wall as a model. Students reread interactive writing fluently and then share with class.*
   Students are not prompted to write frequency words in the same order each day.

Figure 5.5 A Five-Day Fluency Focus Plan—Primary

illegible. We use the same procedure for all five words. We may begin the prompted writing by using words from previous weeks. We like students to start with success.

The lesson continues by bringing the group together to plan for interactive writing. We have students talk about a picture that we have mounted. The pictures we use are snapshots of the children or magazine or newspaper photos. If possible, we try to use pictures that are connected in some way so they can be bound together as a book. We construct a page each day. Constructing a page a day for a book asks students to reread as they think about the next page. An early consideration for students is text structure. Do they want a patterned book similar to what they are independently reading?

Students talk about the picture and plan for the writing. Once the group has agreed on the message, the students are involved in an interactive writing lesson. The interactive writing lesson allows Gayle to support her students' word learning within the context of a continuous text. The pace has to move quickly to maintain attention. The students and Gayle write the message together. Gayle asks students to write various parts of the message. She makes decisions on how students will contribute based on what they understand and still confuse. Students get another opportunity to practice frequent words or challenging print cues from reading or writing. Students think in meaningful language units and then learn how to use print conventions to express this meaning.

I vary the lesson format for intermediate-aged learners. My lesson begins

---

Fluency Focus Small-Group Lesson—Primary

- Read selected words from the word wall.
- Write frequent words on wipe-off board.
- Craft a message by discussing a picture.
- Use interactive writing to write the message.
- Reread the message to ensure it states students' intended idea.

Figure 5.6 Fluency Focus Small-Group Lesson—Primary

with a target group of frequent words; this group of words includes new and review words. My list has approximately ten words. I dictate the words to my students, asking them to "Write _____ quickly and neatly. Then check to make sure you have written the word correctly. Write it again. Write it more quickly. Write it one more time, even more quickly and neatly." I ask the students to write these words three or four times. My goal is automaticity. I do not want my students to think about writing or reading this word. If a student does make a mistake I use a wipe-off board and write the correct spelling for

---

A Five-Day Fluency Focus Plan—Intermediate

Day 1 *Students are prompted to write five frequency words on wipe-off boards. Students work on handwriting and writing the word quickly. Students are supplied a model to monitor accuracy and to self-correct if needed. Students erase the frequent words and write a sentence using one of the high frequency words they are prompted to use. Students read their sentences orally, practicing fluency.*

Day 2 *Students are prompted to write five frequency words from day 1 on wipe-off boards. Students check each others' work. Students write two new frequency words. A model is provided to monitor accuracy and to self-correct if needed. Students erase frequent words and write a sentence using any of the frequency words. Students read their sentences orally, practicing fluency.*

Day 3 *Students are prompted to write the previously introduced frequency words quickly and neatly. A model is provided to students who need one to monitor accuracy and then to self-correct. Students write two new frequency words. Students erase frequent words and write a sentence using one of the two new frequency words. Students read their sentences orally, practicing fluency.*

Day 4 *Students are prompted to write the previously introduced frequency words quickly and neatly. Students write a new frequency word. A model is provided to students who need one to monitor accuracy and then to self-correct. Students erase frequent words and write a sentence using the new frequency word. Students read their sentences orally, practicing fluency.*

Day 5 *Students are prompted to write all the frequency words quickly and neatly. Students write a paragraph using as many of the frequency words as possible. Students read their paragraphs orally, practicing fluency.*

  Students are not prompted to write frequency words in the same order each day.

Figure 5.7 A Five-Day Fluency Focus Plan—Intermediate

the child. They then quickly copy the correct spelling, noting their miscue and where they will pay more attention the next time. Words I choose for students to write fluently come from the 500 high-frequency words and some content words students are using frequently.

Once students have written the entire group of words, I ask them to use one word in a sentence. The students write a sentence using a frequent word. The students then share their sentences by reading them orally to the group. The group assesses whether the sentence makes sense and how fluent the student read it. The students use our class-made fluency rubric (see Appendix).

Fluency Focus Small-Group Lesson—Intermediate

- Write frequent words on wipe-off board.
- Write a sentence using one of the frequent words.
- Read sentence fluently to group.
- Group assesses fluency.
- Reread sentence if not fluent.

Figure 5.8 Fluency Focus Small-Group Lesson—Intermediate

Pump Up the Writing

Once students are able to get their thoughts down in first draft form, we teach them to pump up their writing. When we use the metaphor "pump it up," we are triggering students to think about making their writing more interesting, clear, or detailed, or for them to elaborate. Students learn how to revise their writing by thinking about their word choice and word order, eventually applying these strategies to their first draft writing. Since Gayle and I both have our students keep writing notebooks, our lessons are similar.

We begin the "pumping up" lesson by having our students reread their writing notebook, looking for an idea or sentence they want to "pump up." Students who select an idea craft it quickly into a sentence on a clean page. Students who select a sentence to work with copy it on a clean page. Next, students sit next to a person they trust and work well with, one who will help them think about revising their writing. The students turn and face each other, sitting knee to knee. One child states a goal for writing and then reads the sentence orally to his or her partner. The partner listens to the message and helps the child decide on places the writing can be revised so it is more interesting and clear or could have more detail to help the reader understand the idea.

In my fifth-grade classroom, once my students are comfortable with the process of sharing, getting feedback, and using the feedback as a tool for revision, I add another wrinkle. Students read through writing notebook entries, finding a simple sentence that they want to pump up. Students copy the simple sentence onto a clean page. Students turn knee to knee and read the sentence to their partner. This time the discussion is on the idea. Once both students have orally read their sentences, they write a compound sentence. Next, they use the same reading procedure and write a complex sentence. Students share their sentences in groups of four, reading the three sentences orally, receiving feedback about their writing and getting one more chance to practice fluent reading.

"Pump it up" lessons are periodically used as mini-lessons for writing workshop. These same lessons can be used while students are writing in content areas. We have found that we can use the "pump it up" ideas in small-group work and conferences because students are comfortable with the routines of the lesson. Students are developing both writing stamina and fluency from these lessons as they learn a strategy that helps them move from an idea to written words. When students are thinking of crafting words, they are considering the audience, making their writing clear and interesting, and thinking about sentence length and type to accomplish this goal.

Pinnell and Fountas (1998) remind us of the relationship between word knowledge and fluency. "The rate and fluency of the reading is a good indicator of the reader's ability to quickly solve words." Automaticity with words enables students to read in phrased, meaningful units. Using writing to help students think in meaningful units and learn frequent words is an instructional means to developing fluent readers and writers.

Final Thoughts

We are continuously fine-tuning our thinking and fluency teaching. We have discovered over the years that reading aloud to students, allowing time for students to read "just-right books," rereading a variety of texts, writing to learn throughout the day, and having a systematic word study system have helped our students to develop skills and strategies for reading and writing with fluency. Our students use the idea "bringing words to life" as a synonym for fluent reading. Our fluency instruction has evolved because we are more conscious of our teaching strategies, prompting and calling students' attention to fluent reading and supporting students as they read ideas.

We were recently asked, "Do you think all students need fluency instruction?" Our reply was, "Yes and no." Yes, all students need to hear their teacher read aloud well-crafted texts. Our students need to hear us use our voice as a tool to bring texts to life. They need to hear us change the pace of our reading as we encounter challenging ideas and hard-to-pronounce words. Our students need to hear us reread a text, pondering the author's choice of words, word groups, or punctuation, or how we misread the text.

No, all our students do not need some of the small-group lessons that we use. These small-group lessons are temporary interventions designed to help students read lines of print, read with prosody, or learn about the printer's code so they can use their energy and mind to unearth ideas and read to understand. Writing lessons help our students fluently record their ideas, and then "pump it up" to express their thinking and stories. We want our students to spend most of their school day reading and writing, developing fluency, reading fluently, using literacy as a tool and life-long skill like Aaron has.

The following lessons focus on using assessments in targeted instruction.

Lesson 5.1
Reading with Phrasing: Prosody

Thoughts: When reading a text, we read in meaningful chunks. These units of meaning may be grouped in paragraphs, sentences, phrases, or clauses. The grouping of ideas helps us understand the text. We want our students to read the same way, in meaningful units. Students who are having difficulty with fluency do not read ideas; their focus is on words. To help these students, we guide them to reading ideas by using short texts.

Planning

Select a group of students that you have assessed as reading words, not meaningful units.

Prepare a short text as a copy for an overhead or a chart, or make individual copies for students.

What it looks and sounds like

We have found that introducing this lesson using a familiar text helps students internalize the idea of reading in meaningful units. By using a story or picture book read during read-aloud, we activate schema and guide students in reading ideas. We copy the text so that students can read the text orally.

"Today we are going to read this passage together. While we are reading, we are going to make our voices sound like we are telling a story. We are going to read ideas, so we need to think about important words to emphasize and look at punctuation." This prompt prepares students for the choral reading. (It is important that students have heard you use this language prior to this activity while reading aloud.) Then chorally read the text.

During the choral reading, drop your voice out, using it to keep the pacing, phrasing, or intonation focused on meaning. After reading the passage, we use the prompt, "What did you notice about our reading?" During the debriefing, we reread parts of the text, focusing on phrased meaningful reading to help the group use the meaning of the text to guide their reading.

We bring closure by asking the students, "How will you use your voice to make your reading sound like you are telling a story?" If using nonfiction, we adjust our question, asking, "How will you use your voice to make your reading sound like you are recalling information?"

Lesson 5.2
Fluency in a Flash

Thoughts: Automaticity with print and fluency are synonymous. Students need to read high frequency words automatically as they fluently read texts. Automaticity with print allows students to use their minds to think about the ideas, anticipate ideas, summarize what they are understanding, and reflect on important ideas. Teaching students to read high frequency words automatically is a key component of fluent reading.

Planning

Assess students' reading and/or writing to determine instructional needs.

Construct a word wall with high frequency words and use flash cards.

Students need to be able to see the word wall so they can use it as a tool for learning high frequency words.

What it looks and sounds like

We want our students to read high frequency words in a flash. To help students accomplish this goal we use our word walls and word cards. These are very short and rapidly moving lessons. You can fit them into any part of the day.

We begin by gathering a group of students in front of the word wall. "Today we are going to read words in a flash. Chorally read the words on the wall while I point to them." These prompts focus students' attention and provide a purpose for the activity. We target five words for instruction, then point to the words quickly as students read them chorally in a flash. Once students are familiar with the routine of this activity and other words on the wall, we point to other words on the word wall to help students read high frequency words in a flash.

We then read words cards in a flash. "Now we are going to read the words on the word cards quickly. When I flash the word, chorally read the word." We then flash the five words that have been targeted and previously introduced. We mix them up, prompting students to pick up the pace.

We assess the effectiveness of these lessons by listening to students' oral reading and noting fluency, pacing, and the type of words students pause to process. We also look at students' writing to monitor their spelling of the words. If they are having difficulty, we then use the following lesson, "Frequent Words."

Lesson 5.3
Frequent Words

Thoughts: Students' spelling can give clues to how they are perceiving print. Looking at students' spelling confusions along with reading miscues provides a window into how students look at and recall words. Students who struggle with high frequency words in their reading and writing can benefit from repeated exposure to this lesson format.

Planning

Assess students' reading and writing to determine instructional needs.

Construct a word wall with high frequency words and prepare flash cards.

Students need to be able to see the word wall so they can use it as a tool for learning high frequency words.

Collect wipe-off boards.

What it looks and sounds like

We want our students to read and write high frequency words automatically. Some students need specific instruction designed to help them read and write words fluently so they can think about the ideas they are reading and writing. This lesson is short and moves at a brisk pace. Targeting five words at first and moving up to ten words is a goal for this lesson.

We begin by gathering the students in front of the word wall (primary) or in a circle (intermediate) with word cards. Pointing to the high frequency words on the word wall and having students chorally read them or quickly reading word cards focuses students' attention on word shapes.

Then we use wipe-off boards for students to quickly write these same words and words we have previously introduced. We dictate the words to the students and prompt them, "Write _____ quickly. Write it again more quickly. Write it again, more neatly and more quickly." This helps students focus their attention on working towards automaticity and fluency.

Lesson 5.4
Self-Monitoring: Pacing

Thoughts: Reading logs have been a tool our students have used while reading independently. Peter Johnston's thinking (2005, p. 684) has influenced our reading logs' transformation, "Classroom assessment can socialize children into monitoring and guiding their own literacy learning."

As we have fine-tuned our reading logs, we have adjusted their use so that our students can learn about themselves as readers, especially their reading pace. Having students monitor their own reading pace daily and using this for daily and weekly goals has helped our students increase their reading pace and fluency.

Planning

Students use an independent reading book.

Each needs a sticky note.

Students use their reading logs.

What it looks and sounds like

Students bring the book they are currently reading during independent reading. "Today we are going to read for five minutes. I want you to keep track of how many pages you read during that time." Students read silently for five minutes.

When the five-minute period passes, we prompt our students, "Please stop your reading, mark your spot, and count how many pages you read." The students record the number of pages and date on the sticky note.

Our debriefing discussion covers many areas. These include the part of the book they are reading (the beginning is slower as they are introduced to ideas and characters and understand the setting), rereading (they reread because they are confused, needed to find out what they had read the day before, or went back because they had missed something important earlier in the story), and vocabulary (it was challenging so they had to use a strategy to infer the meaning of an unfamiliar word).

Students then estimate how many pages they should be able to read in thirty minutes. Students write their prediction in their reading logs and then read silently. Once silent reading is finished, students note the number of pages read, relating it to their goal. We spend three to five days using this framework as we help students learn about themselves as readers and their reading pace.

Oral Storytelling Rubric

4 *The speaker spoke in smooth phrases using expression.*
   Ideas flowed, one after the other.
   It was easy to understand what the speaker was talking about.

3 *The speaker talked fast, sometimes putting all their words*
      together, making it hard to follow parts of the story.
   Most of the ideas flowed together.
   We only asked a couple questions to help us understand.

2 *The speaker was choppy, putting a few words together at*
      a time.
   Some of the ideas flowed together, but the speaker paused, trying
      to connect ideas.
   The speaker stuttered, using "um, um" or "like" to connect ideas.
   We had to ask the speaker a lot of questions to help us
      understand.

1 *The speaker sounded like a robot, talking word by word.*
   Ideas were mixed up.
   It was hard to follow the story.

Fluency Rubric

4   *Fluent*

_____   Reads meaningful ideas or phrases

_____   Reads at a good pace

_____   Uses punctuation to guide meaningful phrased reading

_____   Adjusts reading rate to process challenging concepts or unfamiliar words

_____   Uses voice to expressively interpret text

3   *Progressing Toward Fluency*

_____   Reads mostly meaningful ideas or phrases with some word-by-word reading

_____   Reads at an adequate pace

_____   Uses punctuation most of the time to guide meaningful phrased reading; occasionally reads through commas or end punctuation

_____   Adjusts reading rate to process challenging concepts or unfamiliar words by stopping or reading text word-by-word

_____   Uses voice to expressively interpret text most of time

2   *Beginning to Read Phrases/Ideas*

_____   Reads some phrases, but mostly two or three words at a time, sounding choppy; rereads part of the text in meaningful chunks once ideas are processed

_____   Reads at a slow pace

_____   Uses some end punctuation, but may connect one sentence to the next, especially when the sentence ends at the beginning of the next line

_____   Reads through punctuation at times, causing the meaning to change

_____   Processes challenging words and ideas by stopping, sounding out the words, occasionally rereading, and using the meaning and syntax of the text

_____   Uses voice to show expression at the end of the sentence while noticing end punctuation; reading voice is mostly monotone

1   *Word-By-Word Reading*

_____   Reads most of the text word by word

_____   Reads at a labored pace

_____   Reads each word, not attending to the syntax or punctuation of the text; there may be some word groupings, but they are often a sign of picking up the reading pace

_____   Processes challenging words by sounding out unfamiliar words; may read a concept as a meaningful phrase if it is familiar

_____   Voice is mostly monotone, but may show excitement at the end of a sentence when encountering an exclamation point

110

Known High-Frequency Words

List 1

Name _____

Word	Can Read	Can Write
a		
at		
am		
an		
and		
can		
come		
do		
go		
he		
I		
in		
is		
it		
like		
look		
me		
my		
no		
see		
she		
so		
the		
to		
up		
we		

List 2

Name _____

Word	Can Read	Can Write
all		
are		
as		
be		
but		
came		
for		
from		
get		
got		
had		
has		
have		
her		
him		
his		
if		
of		
on		
there		
they		
this		
was		
with		
you		
your		

111

Reading Log

Name _____

Title of Text	Big Idea(s)	Reading Pace
Monday _____		Page Started _____ Page Ended _____ ☐ Good ☐ Needs Improvement
Tuesday _____		Page Started _____ Page Ended _____ ☐ Good ☐ Needs Improvement
Wednesday _____		Page Started _____ Page Ended _____ ☐ Good ☐ Needs Improvement
Thursday _____		Page Started _____ Page Ended _____ ☐ Good ☐ Needs Improvement
Friday _____		Page Started _____ Page Ended _____ ☐ Good ☐ Needs Improvement

Reading Log

Name _____   Date(s) _____

Day	Title(s)	Reading Completed	Genre	Thinking/Comments
Monday		_____ Books _____ Pages	Fiction Nonfiction Poetry	
Tuesday		_____ Books _____ Pages	Fiction Nonfiction Poetry	
Wednesday		_____ Books _____ Pages	Fiction Nonfiction Poetry	
Thursday		_____ Books _____ Pages	Fiction Nonfiction Poetry	
Friday		_____ Books _____ Pages	Fiction Nonfiction Poetry	

BIBLIOGRAPHY

Professional References

Allington, R. 2001. *What Really Matters for Struggling Readers.* New York: Addison-Wesley Educational Publishers, Inc.

Bodrova, E. & Leong, D. 1996. *Tools of the Mind.* Newark: Prentice-Hall, Inc.

Borland, H. 1985. *Hal Borland's Twelve Moons of the Year.* Boston: G. K. Hall & Co.

Clay, M. 1991. *Becoming Literate: The Construction of Inner Control.* Portsmouth, NH: Heinemann.

Collins, B. 2003. *Poetry 180: A Turning Back to Poetry.* New York: Random House.

Ehri, L. C. 1998. "Grapheme-phoneme knowledge is essential for learning to read words in English." In J. L. Metsala & L. C. Ehri (eds.), *Word Recognition in Beginning Literacy* (pp. 3–40). Mahaw, NJ: Erlbaum.

Fletcher, R. and Portalupi, J. 2001. *Writing Workshop: The Essential Guide.* Portsmouth, NH: Heinemann

Fried, R. 2001.*The Passionate Teacher.* Boston: Beacon Press.

Goodman, K. 1970. "Reading: A Psycholinguistic Guessing Game." In H. Singer, R. B. Ruddell, and M. Ruddell, eds. *Theoretical Models and Processes of Reading.* Newark, Delaware: International Reading Association.

Holdaway, D. 1979. *The Foundations of Literacy.* New York :Ashton Scholastic

Johnston, P. 2005. "Literacy assessment and the future." *The Reading Teacher.* Volume 58, No. 7, April 2005, pp. 684–686.

Kuhn, M. 2004. "Helping Students Become Accurate, Expressive Readers: Fluency Instruction for Small Groups." *The Reading Teacher.* Volume 58, No. 4, Dec 2004/Jan 2005.

Lattimer, H. 2003. *Thinking Through Genre: Units of Study in Reading and Writing Workshops 4–12.* Portland, ME: Stenhouse Publishers

Miller, D. 2002. *Reading with Meaning: Teaching Comprehension in the Primary Grades.* Portland, ME: Stenhouse.

Murray, D. 2002.*Write to Learn, Seventh Edition.* Canada: Heinle/Thomson Learning, Inc.

National Reading Panel. 2000. *Teaching Children to Read: An Evidence-Based Assessment of the Scientific Research Literature on Reading and Its Implications for Reading Instruction.* Washington, DC: US Department of Health and Human Services, National Institute of Health.

Pinnell, G. S. & Fountas I. 1998. *Word Matters: Teaching Phonics and Spelling in the Reading/Writing Classroom.* Portsmouth, NH: Heinemann.

Rasinski, T. 1990. "Investigating Measures of Reading Fluency." *Educational Reading Quarterly,* 14(3), 37–44.

———— 2003. *The Fluent Reader: Oral Reading Strategies for Building Word Recognition, Fluency, and Comprehension.* New York: Scholastic.

Routman, R. 2003. *Reading Essentials: The Specifics You Need to Teach Reading Well.* Portsmouth, NH: Heinemann.

Samuels, S. J. 1979. "The Method of Repeated Readings." *The Reading Teacher,* Vol. 32, 403–408.

Shanahan, B. 2004. *Ohio Journal of English Language Arts,* Volume 44 Number 2, pp. 31–38.

Smith, F. 1988. *Joining the Literacy Club.* Portsmouth, NH: Heinemann.

Stahl, K. 2003. *The Effects of Three Instructional Methods on the Reading Comprehension and Content Acquisition of Novice Readers.* Unpublished doctoral dissertation. The University of Georgia, Athens.

Stanovich, K. E. 1980. "Toward an Interactive-Compensatory Model of Individual Differences in the Development of Reading Fluency." *Reading Research Quarterly,* 16, pp. 32–71.

Tierney, R. J. and Readance, J. E., 1990. *Reading Strategies and Practices: A Compendium.* Boston: Allyn & Bacon.

Truss, L. 2003. *Eats, Shoots & Leaves: The Zero Tolerance Approach to Punctuation.* New York: Gotham Books.

Worthy, J., Broaddus, K., and Ivey, M. 2001. *Pathways to Independence: Reading, Writing, and Learning in Grades 3–8.* New York: Guilford.

Zutell, J., and Rasinski, T. 1991. "Training Teachers to Attend to Their Students' Oral Reading Fluency." *Theory into Practice,* 30, pp. 211–217.

Children's Literature

Adler, D. *Cam Jansen.* Puffin Books: New York.

Adoff, A. 1986. *Sports Pages.* New York: J. B. Lippincott

Algie, A. 1997. *The Tea Party.* Denver: Shortland Publications.

Borden, L. 2004. *Sea Clocks: The Story of Longitude.* New York: Margaret McElderry Books.

Bruchac, J. 2004. *Hidden Roots.* New York: Scholastic.

Cairns, S. 1987. *Oh No!* Chicago: Rigby.

Cowley, J. 1983. *The Jigaree.* Canada: The Wright Group.

———— 1993. *Where are you going, Aja Rose?* Bothell, WA: The Wright Group

———— 1993. *Bread.* Bothell, WA: The Wright Group

———— 2000. *Mud Walk.* Canada: The Wright Group.

Creech, S. 1996. *Walk Two Moons.* New York: Harper Trophy

Cronin, D. 2003. *Diary of a Worm.* New York: HarperCollins.

Giff, P. R. 2002. *Pictures of Hollis Woods.* New York: Wendy Lamb Books.

Graves, D. 1996. "Rabbit" and "The Night Before Fishing Season Opens" from *Baseball, Snakes, and Summer Squash: Poems About Growing Up.* Honesdale, PA: Boyds Mills Press.

Laminack, L. 2004. *Saturdays & Teacakes.* Atlanta, GA: Peachtree Publishers, LTD.

Lobel,A. *Frog and Toad* A series of books. New York : Harper & Row

Martin, A. 2001. *Belle Teal.* New York: Scholastic.

Munsch, R., and Martchenko, M. 1985. *Mortimer.* Canada: Annick Press Ltd.

Price, H. L. 1999. *These Hands.* New York: Hyperion Books for Children.

Rylant, C. *Henry and Mudge in Puddle Trouble.* New York: Harcourt Brace & Company.

Schaefer, L. 2001. *Simple Machines*. New York: Benchmark Education Company.

Seinfeld, J. 2002. *Halloween*. Boston: Little, Brown.

Shannon, D. 1998. *No, David!* New York: The Blue Sky Press.

Singer, M. 1994. *Turtle in July*. New York: Simon and Schuster.

Stevens, J. 1987. *The Three Billy Goats Gruff*. New York: Harcourt Brace & Company.

Time for Kids. "After the Waves" February 4, 2005.

Walter, V. 1995. *"Hi, Pizza Man!"* New York: Orchard Books.

Wood, D. & A. 1984. *The Little Mouse, The Red Ripe Strawberry, and THE BIG HUNGRY BEAR*. Singapore: Child's Play.

Woodson, J. 2001.*The Other Side*. New York: Putnam.